Lady Lytton's Court Diary

LADY LYTTON

Lady Lytton's Court Diary

1895–1899

EDITED BY

Mary Lutyens

RUPERT HART-DAVIS
SOHO SQUARE LONDON
1961

Made and printed in Great Britain by
William Clowes and Sons, Limited, London and Beccles

Contents

6 *Contents*

Illustrations

Foreword

MY grandmother, Lady Lytton, was a Lady-in-Waiting to Queen Victoria and to Queen Alexandra from 1895 to 1905. For the first four years she kept a record of her life at Court in the form of a diary written in exercise books. The diary is very slight and adds only a few grains to the vast dune of Victoriana, but for those of us who are fascinated by the period every grain is a treasure, and the very flatness of Lady Lytton's style more clearly reveals the great little old lady in the last and least well-documented years of her reign.

Lady Lytton was a bad speller, particularly of French, and she often misspelt proper names. These, as well as her other spelling mistakes I have corrected to avoid confusion, and I have put in punctuation where the meaning was not clear. Information about those mentioned in the book who are not listed in readily available reference books will be found in the Biographical Index if not given in the text.

I have to acknowledge the gracious permission of Her Majesty the Queen to publish extracts from Queen Victoria's journal. I am deeply grateful to Mr Mackworth-Young, the Librarian of the Royal Library at Windsor, and to his assistant, Miss Olwen Hedley, for their great kindness in helping me to identify some of the people mentioned in the diary and for certain information they have given me. I am also indebted to Mrs John Orr, Lady Mary Baring, Lady Reid, Mrs Osbert Lancaster, Sir John Forbes, Sir Archibald Edmonstone, Lord Balfour of Burleigh, Dr John Lamb (Minister of Crathie), the Bishop of Nice, Colonel McGhie (Officer Commanding the Royal Victoria Hospital, Netley), Professor Truchanovshi (Director of the Moscow Institute of History), the Spanish and American Embassies, Mr John

H. Scholes of the British Transport Commission, Mr Harold Tarrant (Clerk of the Old Etonian Association) and the Town Clerk of Edinburgh for their help in making identifications; and to the editorial department of Debrett and Messrs Thomas Cook for their kind help.

I am most grateful to the following for permission to quote copyright material: Lord Ponsonby of Shulbrede and Messrs Macmillan for *Henry Ponsonby* by Arthur Ponsonby; The Hon. Mrs Miller Jones and Messrs Ernest Benn for *Lord James of Hereford* by Lord Askwith; Air Vice-Marshal Arthur Gould Lee and Messrs Faber and Faber for *The Empress writes to Sophie*; Messrs George Allen and Unwin for *Queen Mary* by James Pope-Hennessy; Messrs Longmans Green for *Edward Marsh* by Christopher Hassall; Messrs John Murray for *The Letters of Queen Victoria*; Messrs Eyre and Spottiswoode for *Recollections of Three Reigns* by Sir Frederick Ponsonby; Messrs the Bodley Head for *Letters of the Tsar to the Tsaritsa*; Messrs Gerald Duckworth for *Letters from the Tsaritsa to the Tsar*; and Messrs Evans Brothers for *My Memories of Six Reigns* by Princess Marie Louise.

M.L.

Chapter One

My dear Lady Lytton,

A vacancy has occurred amongst my ladies-in-waiting caused by an event, which has grieved me deeply, viz., the death of my dear & valued friend the Dow^{gr} Duchess of Roxburgh, and I w^d like to offer it to you.

Having known so many of y^r family for so long, several of them having been, & still being in my household, & having a grateful sense of y^r husband's distinguished services, as well as a sincere admiration of the way in which you have borne y^r sorrows & trials, it w^d give me much pleasure if you w^d accept this offer.

Hoping soon to hear from you,

Believe me always y^s affec^{tly},

Victoria R.I.

Edith Lytton was fifty-four and had been a widow for three and a half years when this offer was made to her by Queen Victoria. Her husband, Robert, first Earl of Lytton, had died in November 1891, while Ambassador in Paris. They had married in 1864 when he was First Secretary at Lisbon and was still contemplating giving up diplomacy to devote himself to writing poetry. He had already had three books of poems published under the *nom de plume* of Owen Meredith. They had been very well received, but quick promotion, the financial demands of an increasing family as well as opposition from his father, Bulwer Lytton, had kept him in the Diplomatic Service, though he continued to write in his spare time. In 1876 he was appointed Viceroy of India on the recommendation of Lord Beaconsfield, his father's old friend, and it was he who conducted the Durbar at which Queen Victoria was proclaimed Empress of India in 1877.

All his letters to the Queen from India were written in the first person, a privilege accorded him after his first letter to her written thus in ignorance of the etiquette which then required the third person when addressing the Sovereign. She always wrote to him, however, in the third person, so her letter to Lady Lytton may seem particularly gracious (she wrote only once in the first person to Sir Henry Ponsonby, her Private Secretary, during the whole course of their long association and that was at the death of his mother), but on personal matters she always wrote in the first person, to both ladies and gentlemen.

Lord Lytton resigned in 1880 when Lord Beaconsfield's Government fell. His administration was much criticised by the Opposition although the Queen herself defended and up-held him. After some years of retirement he was appointed to Paris in 1887.

He died of cerebral thrombosis, and the Queen wrote in her journal on 24 November 1891: "Most dreadfully shocked at hearing that Lord Lytton died suddenly this afternoon at Paris. For the last three years, at Biarritz, Aix and Grasse he had always come to see me, and was ever kind, loyal and chivalrous. I see him now in my mind, sitting in the little drawing-roon at Grasse, talking to me of all manner of things."

Edith Lytton was the daughter of Edward Villiers (a brother of Lord Clarendon) and Elizabeth Liddell, ninth of the sixteen children of Lord Ravensworth. Edith had two sisters, one of them her twin, and one brother. Her father died when she was two, and her mother was left very badly off. If it had not been for the kindness of Lord Clarendon in putting a house on his own estate at their disposal the family would have been in great want.

Edith and her sisters received little formal education. They had no resident governess and were instructed in music and drawing by visiting masters. However, they went abroad every year for the sake of economy and their mother's health, and after they came out were able to listen to the talk of the great at their Uncle Clarendon's table.

Robert and Edith had had seven children, but their eldest, a boy, had died when he was six, and a second boy, born after the birth of two girls, died at eighteen months. A third girl followed, and then, while they were in India, two boys, the elder of whom, Victor, was the Queen's godson and succeeded to the title on the death of his father.[1]

In May 1895, when Lady Lytton was appointed a Lady-in-Waiting, the eldest daughter, Betty, was twenty-eight and married to Gerald Balfour, a brother of Arthur Balfour; Constance and Emily, twenty-six and twenty, were unmarried and living at home; Victor, who was going to be nineteen, was preparing to go up to Cambridge, while the youngest boy Neville, sixteen, was still at Eton. Eighteen months after Lord Lytton's death, the man of business to whom Lord Lytton had entrusted large sums of money failed completely and the family income was reduced to £1900 a year, including the money given by the estate for Victor's education. Strict economies became essential. Knebworth House, the family home in Hertfordshire, was fortunately let; the expense of London life was out of the question, so Lady Lytton rented a small house called the Danes about twelve miles from Knebworth.

The post of Lady-in-Waiting would bring in £300 a year, and yet Lady Lytton did not accept the Queen's offer without some heart-searching. Would her husband have approved was the question she must ask herself? A submissive as well as an utterly devoted wife, she had looked to him as her judge and her conscience in all things. It would be simpler and perhaps better if it could be arranged for her daughter Emily to become a Maid-of-Honour, for that would also bring in £300 a year, but Emily indignantly turned down the suggestion and declared that she was a republican.

---

[1] The story of Robert and Edith's courtship and marriage, and the birth of their eldest son, is told in *The Birth of Rowland* by Lady Emily Lutyens, while a vivid account of the Lytton family in the nineties is given in the same author's *A Blessed Girl*.

In the end her son-in-law, Gerald Balfour, on whom she relied greatly, persuaded her that her husband would certainly have approved, for otherwise it might not be possible to keep Neville on at Eton. But it was not until October that she took up her new duties.

October 1895 at Balmoral. The Queen was seventy-six; she was very lame and her sight was failing, and yet she was probably happier now than she had been at any time since the Prince Consort's death in 1861. Her youngest daughter Beatrice and her four children lived with her and the Princess's husband, Prince Henry of Battenberg, had brought sweetness and sunshine into her life. The Queen loved male society, and Prince Henry, who was a naturalised Englishman, was always at hand to help her with family problems and with her more intimate letters. She was closer to her grandchildren and more lenient with them than she had been with any of her children (except Beatrice, the youngest, who had never left her and had been her chief consolation after Albert's death), and the company and concerns of the Battenberg children were a constant interest and delight to her.[1]

Another grand-daughter, Victoria, the eldest child of her daughter Princess Alice of Hesse who had died of diphtheria at the age of thirty-five, had married Henry of Battenberg's brother, Louis, in the disconcerting way the Royal family had of marrying out of their generation, so that Princess Beatrice's niece was not only her sister-in-law but the wife of her husband's *eldest* brother. Prince Louis, also naturalised, was an Admiral in the British Navy, and this Battenberg pair and their children (Queen Victoria's *great*-grandchildren but no younger than her Battenberg grandchildren) were also very dear to her. The eldest little girl, described by the Empress Frederick as being "quite lovely," was destined to become the mother of Prince Philip.

The Queen's third daughter, Princess Helena, invariably known as Princess Christian, was married to Prince Christian of Schleswig-Holstein, yet another naturalised Englishman

[1] A letter from the Queen expressing her attitude towards her own children is given in Appendix A on p. 155.

and a General in the British Army, and they lived close to her at Windsor in Cumberland Lodge. Their elder daughter, Princess Helena Victoria, was a great favourite with the Queen and often stayed with her at Osborne and Balmoral.

The family tragedy of 1892, the death from pneumonia of the Prince of Wales's eldest son, the Duke of Clarence, was now almost forgotten in its happy aftermath. His fiancée, Princess May of Teck, had married his brother, George, Duke of York, and on 23 June 1894 a son had been born to them, Prince Edward.

The Queen's greatest trial in 1895 was the retirement of Sir Henry Ponsonby who had been in her Household for thirty-eight years, first as Equerry to the Prince Consort and then for the last twenty-five years as her Private Secretary and Keeper of the Privy Purse. In January he had had a stroke which had deprived him of the power of speech, and in May he had been obliged to send in his resignation. He was only sixty-nine but had worn himself out in her service. The physical labour alone of having to write every letter and dispatch by hand must have been immense, and to add to his work the Queen demanded that even when he was under the same roof, every communication with her should be written down in the form of a memorandum with all the clumsiness of the third person address. This time-consuming practice of writing notes to people staying in the same house was adopted by the entire Household.

The Queen did not feel Sir Henry's loss quite as much as she might have done, however, because Lieutenant-Colonel Bigge, who had been trained under Sir Henry for fifteen years, was there to succeed him; and there was Sir Fleetwood Edwards, also trained under Sir Henry, to take over the Privy Purse. Arthur Bigge had first been introduced into the Royal Household as Equerry by the Empress Eugénie. He had been attached to the same battalion at Aldershot as the Prince Imperial and had been his greatest friend, and after the Prince's death in the Zulu War of 1879 he was taken up by the Empress. Very soon after his appointment as Private Secretary he was knighted by the Queen on her birthday, 24 May 1895. He was raised to the peerage as

Lord Stamfordham in 1911 and was to remain in the service
of the Royal Family until his death in 1931.

So much for the domestic scene. Affairs of state were
equally conducive to the Queen's contentment. Mr Gladstone
had retired; the short-lived Unionist Government under
Lord Rosebery had been defeated in June over the seemingly
trivial matter of keeping an insufficient amount of cordite
ammunition for the Army, and now the Queen's old friend,
Lord Salisbury, at the age of sixty-five, was back for the
third time as Prime Minister. He also held the office of
Foreign Secretary, with Joseph Chamberlain, one of the
four Liberal Unionists in the Cabinet, as Colonial Secretary.

There was usually a Minister in Attendance at Balmoral,
but it was so dull and cold there that the Ministers dreaded
having to go. (Lord James of Hereford described it as
"cold as death.") The Court, wherever it was, was nearly
always in mourning, and the papers were full of advertise-
ments for "Fashionable Mourning" and "Waterproof
Crape." In 1895 ladies still wore the leg-of-mutton sleeve,
the feather boa, curled fringe, tiny hat or bonnet tied under
the chin and the straw boater for sport, especially for bicycl-
ing which was the latest craze. During the period covered by
Lady Lytton's diary, figures grew gradually more and more
streamlined and apparently taller and taller, hair more and
more puffed out, and hats larger and larger, until there
emerged, by 1899, the stately Edwardian silhouette we
know so well. Lady Lytton had been dressed by Worth
when she was in Paris and her new appointment made it
again possible for her to have her clothes from Worth, and
to have also the comfort of a personal maid, a luxury she
had had to forgo when the financial crash came, and the
one she had missed most. She could have had no misgivings
therefore about her clothes when she went to Balmoral,
but it must have been depressing to go back into mourning.
The ladies surrounding Queen Victoria had been in semi-
mourning since the death of the Prince Consort in 1861.
Until the end of 1862 the Ladies and Gentlemen were
directed to wear mourning on all social occasions, but after
1864 the Queen directed that although she herself would

wear deep black for the rest of her life, and the lady-in-waiting should wear the same, the rest when in waiting might wear grey, violet, lilac or white.[1] The Queen later relaxed this rule for herself to the extent of wearing a white cap, and it was slightly relaxed for the lady-in-waiting also.

And now a word about Balmoral itself. The original house was taken on lease by the Queen and Prince Albert in September 1848 from the Earl of Mar. (There was no railway up Deeside in those days and the main line had not even reached Aberdeen, so the Royal party were obliged to travel either by sea or by carriage from Montrose.) In 1852 they were able to buy the house and estate of over seventeen thousand acres, and the next year the house was demolished and building begun on the present Castle. William Smith of Aberdeen was nominally the architect, but the Queen claimed that it was "my dearest Albert's *own* creation, own work, own building, own laying out as at Osborne." The Prince also designed the Balmoral tartan of black, red and lavender on a grey background.

The Castle is situated on the south side of the River Dee in a long wooded valley between Ballater and Braemar and about nine miles from each. The estate also includes the small eighteenth-century manor house of Birkhall, near Ballater, where the Duchess of Albany, the widow of the Queen's youngest son Leopold, usually stayed with her children in the summer. (The Queen Mother now stays at Birkhall.) Abergeldie Castle, five miles from Balmoral, was held on lease, had been occupied in former days by the Duchess of Kent, the Queen's mother, and was at this time lent to distinguished visitors such as the widowed Empress Eugénie who was staying there during Lady Lytton's first waiting.[2]

Between the two Castles is the kirk at Crathie. (John Brown is buried in the churchyard there.) Prominent Scottish preachers were called in to deliver the sermon, and two communion services were held there every year, one in

---

[1] This information is received from the Librarian at Windsor.

[2] Abergeldie is still held on lease by the Crown, the owner refusing to sell, but the beautiful Castle has fallen into such disrepair that it is uninhabitable.

2

the spring and one in the autumn. The Queen was much criticised for taking communion in a Scots church but this did not stop her from doing so, although the Deans of Westminster and Windsor as well as the Archbishop of Canterbury advised her against it.[1] The old white-washed kirk of 1805 was pulled down in 1893 and a larger building, designed by Dr Marshall Mackenzie, put in its place. The Queen was present at the laying of the foundation stone of the new church and at its opening and dedication on 18 June 1895, a fortnight after her letter to Lady Lytton.

And so the scene is set for Lady Lytton's first journey to Balmoral to take up her new duties. The country was familiar to her because as a girl of eighteen she had stayed with Lord Dudley, when he was still Lord Ward, at a shooting-box, Corndavon Lodge, which he had rented not far from Balmoral. Lord Ward had proposed to her there, but as he was twenty-six years older than she was, her mother, who had herself had a romance with him in her widowhood, prevented the marriage.

When Lady Lytton arrived at Balmoral, Sir Matthew White Ridley, the Home Secretary, was the Minister in Attendance, and the Hon. Harriet Phipps, daughter of Sir Charles Phipps, former Keeper of the Privy Purse, was the Woman-of-the-Bedchamber in waiting. (All the Queen's Bedchamber-Women and untitled Maids-of-Honour were given the rank of Baron's daughter.) Miss Phipps had been with the Queen, first as Maid-of-Honour, then as Woman-of-the-Bedchamber, since 1862, and was very close to her. She was used as a go-between by other members of the Household. Lady Lytton already knew her, for she had met her when she privately presented her daughter Emily to the Queen at Windsor in 1892.[2]

Balmoral Castle. October 1895

I arrived at this Castle for my first waiting on the 3rd of October at about half past three after a bitter cold journey

---

[1] She had been present for the first time at a Communion Service in the kirk at Crathie on 13 November 1871, and from 1873 she regularly partook of the autumn Communion there.

[2] Lady Lytton's account of this presentation is given in Appendix B on p. 156.

from Aberdeen where I slept, having come the day before
from the Danes to catch the ten express from London.
The drive from Ballater was lovely along the Dee and reminded me of the time we were at Corndavon with Lord
Dudley and used to ride about all these roads. I was shown
to my bedroom on arrival on the ground floor, a not very
large room and one could hardly move when the two boxes
were brought in.[1] The carpet is a green sporting Tartan, and
the sofa, chair and curtains white Royal Victoria Tartan and a
glazed chintz. Miss Phipps soon came and then Princess
Christian who was most cordial and kind and took me to her
sitting-room. I went to the billiard-room at five and had to
preside over the teapot for the ladies but only Miss Phipps
was there. There are no maids-of-honour now here as the
German lady, Fräulein Colomb, with Princess Henry of
Prussia,[2] has to have their room.

Miss Phipps told me the Queen would receive me on
coming in from her drive. We waited a little time in her
passage, then I was shown in to the room that was the Prince
Consort's dressing-room which she uses for receiving
upstairs, though formal receptions are held in the drawing-
room downstairs. The Queen looked well but her knees are
very stiff, partly caused by two falls on them. But there is
no pain now left. I thanked her Majesty so much for all her
kindness and she spoke with feeling about all I had gone
through, then asked after Victor and the others and added,
"I was glad to see Lady Betty the other day and so like her
father." I asked the Queen what news she had from India and
after saying it was good, she spoke of Lord Elgin's great
shyness. "He was Lord-in-Waiting one time, and no one
could make him speak and now it is the same in India."

[The 9th Earl of Elgin had been appointed Viceroy in
1894. On 12 August 1893 the Queen had written about him
to Mr Gladstone: "She hardly thinks him well suited for

---

[1] A niece, who visited Lady Lytton in this room, asked her where she wrote
her letters. "On the bed," she replied.

[2] The Queen's grand-daughter, Princess Irène of Hesse, married to her
first cousin, a brother of the Kaiser. Unlike the Kaiser, Prince Henry was very
popular in England.

this important post. He is very shy and most painfully silent, has no presence, no experience whatever in administration. He would not command the respect that is necessary to that office."]

The Queen said after small topicking, "Here is the order for you," and presented me with the case of the Victoria and Albert Order with the white ribbon which her ladies always wear. I thanked gratefully and spoke of her Majesty's letter when giving me the Crown of India Order instituted when we were in India. "Now I wish to have my tea," and the Queen dismissed me.

I met Princess Beatrice at her door looking very sad after her return journey from her mother-in-law, Princess of Battenberg's, funeral. She told me the next day that she was found dead on the floor of her room from the stroke of apoplexy, or maybe another case of arterial clot.

[The Princess of Battenberg was the morganatic wife of Prince Alexander of Hesse, the youngest son of Lewis II, Grand Duke of Hesse-Darmstadt. Prince Alexander's sister, Marie, had married the Tsarevitch (afterwards Alexander II) in 1841, and her brother as a young man had gone with her to St Petersburg for the wedding and was given a commission in the Russian Army. He was a great favourite at Court until he fell in love with a Polish Countess, Julia von Hauke, Lady-in-Waiting to the Tsarina (Charlotte of Prussia, wife of Nicholas I). The attachment was frowned upon by the Royal family, and as Prince Alexander refused to give up his love, he was obliged to resign his commission and leave Russia. In 1851 he married Julia Hauke but as she was his morganatic wife she could not take his name. However, a title which had been allowed to lapse for five hundred years was conferred upon her by the Grand Duke of Hesse and she became Countess Battenberg—Battenberg being the name of a small town near Darmstadt—and the Castle of Heiligenberg was bequeathed to Prince Alexander by his mother, the Grand Duchess Wilhelmine, who had bought it as a farm-house and converted it into a Schloss.

In 1858 the Countess and her children, consisting of a girl and four boys, were elevated to the rank of Serene Highness by Alexander's brother who had recently succeeded as Grand Duke of Hesse.

The Battenbergs were said to be the handsomest family in Europe. The daughter, Marie, married Count Ernst of Erbach-Schonberg. The eldest son, Prince Louis, married his first cousin once removed, Princess Victoria of Hesse. In 1917 he changed his name to Mountbatten and was created Marquess of Milford Haven. The third son, Prince Henry, married Princess Beatrice and was the father of Queen Ena of Spain and of the Marquess of Carisbrooke; the youngest, Francis Joseph, married Princess Anna of Montenegro. He was often at Queen Victoria's Court where he was extremely popular, although, unlike his brother Henry, he was a very bad shot. It was the second son, though, Prince Alexander, who had the most interesting life. Chosen by the Great Powers after the Congress of Berlin to be Prince of Bulgaria, and later kidnapped by the Russians and forced to abdicate, his career was as adventurous and romantic, both in love and war, as that of any hero in fiction.]

I then went to see where Miss Phipps's room was and had a little talk and she helps me over everything so kindly and brought me back to my room.

At about half past seven the servant knocks and says, "You are invited to dine with the Queen, miladi," and so it will be each night I suppose.[1] Dinner is a nominal nine, but one has to wait in the drawing-room from that time. The only others of the household who dined were Sir Fleetwood Edwards [Keeper of the Privy Purse] (who was leaving the next day), Sir James Reid [the Resident Physician] and Baron von Hahn, with Prince Henry of Prussia. The servant says, "The Queen has arrived," at the door and we stand in the doorway as her Majesty, leaning with her left arm on Mustafa, a small native Indian servant in Indian costume, leads the way, then follow the Princesses, and the Princes make me pass before them.

[1] The Queen's ladies never dined with her unless commanded to do so.

The beginning of dinner was rather solemn, though one talked to one's neighbours all round. The Queen hardly spoke till the middle of dinner when she referred to the Spanish Ambassador having come in the afternoon and expected to be received with the Ambassadress at once without making an appointment, and this was laughed at all round for some little time and all was easy after, and the Princesses Irene of Prussia and Victoria of Schleswig-Holstein [Princess Helena Victoria] were very cheerful and smiling. The evenings are also easy when the party is small. Miss Phipps came in and I watched what she did, to know better what my duties in helping the Queen would be, but I had some talk with the Queen also and she said, "May I be allowed to call you by your Christian name—Edith?" which I was glad of as she does so to her other ladies.

The Princesses play patiences but the gentlemen stand at the end of the room in a very stiff way and very tiring to themselves. About eleven the patiences stop and looks are sent across to the Queen who sits happily in her chair. When she takes her stick, as if by magic the servants outside know it and open the door and Mustafa glides in but without a salaam, seizes the Queen's left arm, and she rises slowly, but still darts across the room when walking. At the door the Princes come and kiss her hand and then the Queen goes away and the Princesses follow.

One feels very idiotic after this, and we either leave the drawing-room direct, or pass through the billiard-room where the other gentlemen of the household remain.

[Dr James Reid had been appointed Resident Physician in 1881. He was an Aberdeenshire man and his home was at Ellon on the east coast. The Queen was very fond of doctors and Dr Reid had a special appeal for her, for not only was he a Scot but also a German scholar. When he was first appointed, however, he did not dine with the Household because the Queen still adhered to the custom of doctors being placed "below the salt," but he was such good company that members of the Household, particularly Sir Henry Ponsonby who became a very close friend of his, took to dining with him whenever they could avoid the Queen's dull dinners. The Queen got to hear that Dr Reid gave "dinner parties" and put a stop to this rival attraction by departing from convention and inviting him to dine with her. By the time Lady Lytton came to Balmoral the doctor was invariably at the Queen's table whenever gentlemen were present. As well as his great qualifications as a doctor he was a man of wide intellect and wit, and the Queen came to rely more and more on his excellent judgement on matters outside his profession. He was knighted in 1895 and created a Baronet in 1897.]

October 4

Dear wedding day which made me wonder if dear Robert would like my present duties for me, but I think it does help me to keep more cheerful, and before the world's eyes is helpful for the family, and the Queen is most kind and my duties for her are very simple. A lovely but cold day and the hills so beautiful I longed to be out climbing them all day. Princess Christian kindly came and asked me to walk with her and she is so nice and easy. She told me of her own weak health and spoke of the Queen's loss of sight, that she had not been able to read a book for two years, but it is the nerves and failure, and can only be helped by prudence, and not using them at night. The grounds are so well kept, and roads very dry.

Miss Phipps told me in the morning the Queen wished me to show the Spanish Ambassadress and her daughter into the drawing-room after luncheon, and then leave them, and I with difficulty learnt their names, La Comtesse de Casa Valencia and Mlle Alcalá Galiano, and then after all said nothing but curtsied and let them pass in. They were very easy nice people and not a vestige of shyness about them. The daughter promised to teach Emmie [her youngest daughter Emily] Spanish dances.[1]

---

[1] The Conde de Casa Valencia was Spanish Ambassador from 1895 to 1898 and had come to Balmoral to present his credentials. His family name was Alcalá Galiano. His daughter did not teach Emily Spanish dances in spite of her promise.

Miss Fraser[1] came to lunch and to see Princess Christian. She is dark and handsome and looks very sad in her deep black for her father's sudden death, and her mother is very odd as usual. When the presentation of the Spaniards to Princess Christian was over we jumped for joy and went for a little drive (having ascertained there were no orders) to write my name on the Empress Eugénie at Abergeldie.

At dinner only Sir Arthur Bigge, just arrived, besides myself and it was all easy and pleasant. Prince Henry of Prussia speaks with authority and seems full of spirit and intelligence and even told "Grandmama" she was not right in something she said about one of his sisters, which surprised the Princess I thought, for Princess Christian always seems rather in awe of "dear Mama." Princess Beatrice and Prince Henry [of Battenberg] dined and they talk much more than they used. I stayed by the Queen and got a good deal of small general talk in the evening. Sir Arthur Bigge talked business rather loud about the new military organisation at headquarters and thinking the Duke of Cambridge's speeches were unwise. But the Queen seemed to be amused to be told details.[2]

October 5

Prince Henry of Battenberg's birthday. Walked with Fräulein Colomb in the morning along by the Dee and it was so pretty and nice and the day less cold and all the roads and paths are beautifully kept. The garden is quite small and uninteresting. We were told at luncheon to receive the Empress Eugénie who was coming at 3.15 and it interested me much, but I was very glad of a thick cloth zouave for we sat on a bench with the hall door open for twenty minutes.

[1] Helena Fraser was a daughter of Lieut.-General James Keith Fraser. Her mother was Amelia Alice, daughter of the Hon. Humble Dudley Ward. In 1898 Miss Fraser married the 3rd Earl of Stradbroke.

[2] The Duke of Cambridge was the Queen's first cousin and almost exactly her own age. He had been fifty-eight years in the Army, thirty-nine of them as Commander-in-Chief. Earlier in the year the Queen had had great trouble in persuading him to retire in favour of Lord Wolseley. He had married, morganatically, an actress, Lucie Farebrother (1815–1890), who became Mrs. Louisa Fitzgeorge; and they lived happily together for almost fifty years although their marriage was never officially recognised. They had three sons.

She came in a brougham with very quick horses and jumped
out as if she was much younger than she is. [She was sixty-
nine.] She shook hands and muttered something about being
pleased to see me and I could see traces of beauty still, but
Princess Beatrice was waiting with Prince Henry so she soon
passed on.

I had been told I was to drive with the Queen and Princess
Christian at four, so I went at once to dress warm as the
order included (from the Scotch Piper who sings his words
and is very difficult to understand) tea at some lodge, and I
knew we should be home late.

Of course more waiting in the library, but Princess
Christian soon came, and always has lots of talk. The
process of getting her Majesty into the carriage is intricate,
with a green baize plank slanting up from the door-step.
Then the Indian servant supports the Queen the most, and so
gently, and without any fear or nervousness, then there were
cloaks, shawls, and frills offered by different hands. Princess
Christian seemed terribly afraid of taking too much room,
and sat right forward and I opposite. Then the many rugs
were brought in turn, and finally a lovely new green rug,
reversible cloth with white plaid the other side. "This was a
present given to me the other day, and a beautiful one,"
the Queen said. At last the two outriders on greys and the
four beautifully driven in hand greys started off. I felt rather
inclined to giggle but not at all alarmed. We went on to the
road to Braemar where I remembered riding so well, and the
Queen told the Princess I had been here as a girl, and it
led to talking of old days. (He [Lord Ward] proposed to me
on that road.) We stopped at a cottage and the Queen gave
a woman a dress so kindly and the small talk never stopped
and when the Queen dozed at times the Princess and I went on
talking. The tea at the head keeper's, Donald Stewart,[1] was
very nice and only Mustafa waited on us, so quickly and

---

[1] Son of Donald Stewart whom the Queen had found as a keeper at Balmoral
in 1848, and who had been much liked by Prince Albert. He had always led the
dogs when the Prince went out stalking. The Western Lodge was built for
him by the Prince. A suite of rooms was set apart in it for the Queen's use, the
tearoom being panelled in polished pine from the forest, and the Balmoral
tartan used for the upholstery.

well, and he is very like my jemadar in India. The scones, Scotch pancakes and jam were all extra perfect, made by Stewart, and we all ate much more than we ought. The drive back was quite short.

The Minister, Sir M. W. Ridley, and Professor Story [Chaplain-in-Ordinary to the Queen] were in the drawing-room for dinner and I knew both so it seemed very nice to have them there, and I sat by Dr Story but Princess Beatrice seemed too pleased to talk with him to spare me much.[1] I heard him speaking of the Duke of Argyll's third marriage as if he could not do without a wife and it had been the same after his first wife's death, but Princess Beatrice said it was very hard for the family. [The Duke of Argyll was the father-in-law of Princess Louise, Marchioness of Lorne. In July, at the age of seventy-two, and a year after the death of his second wife, he had married Ina McNeil, one of the Queen's Maids-of-Honour. On May 27 the Queen had written in her journal, "Received a rather startling letter from the Duke of Argyll, telling me he had proposed to Ina McNeil, whom he had known long and always admired, and she had accepted him, though she felt deeply leaving me." The Duke's father had also married three times in quick succession.]

I stayed by the Queen and talked sometimes and she asked me to bring Sir M. W. Ridley to her and he also told her about business of his office and discussed the rows at Constantinople. [Fresh atrocities against the Armenians had broken out in Turkey, and the Queen discussed with Sir Matthew while he was there the advisability of intervening herself personally with the Sultan. On December 28 she did in fact write and appeal to him "for the cause of humanity" to restore peace.] Dr Story was brought up later. The Queen gives a curious nervous laugh when first people are brought up.

---

[1] Lady Lytton might have felt it even nicer to have Sir Matthew Ridley there had she known that almost exactly twenty-nine years later, his grandson, the 3rd Viscount Ridley, and her grand-daughter, Ursula Lutyens, both as yet unborn, were to be married. Sir Matthew was created a Viscount in 1900. The Very Rev. Robert Herbert Story (1835–1907) was Professor of Church History 1886–98, and Principal of Glasgow University 1898–1900.

Sunday, October 6

There was Scotch Service in the Chapel, and the assembling, waiting and retiring was fearfully solemn. I sat behind the Queen's chair and put the stick in a rest and took it out, and we had no bonnets on, so it did not seem very like church.

Dr Story was very fine in his extempore prayer and sermon, on the Union and Unity of the Church, and very liberal and intellectual and he looked so handsome and was beautifully attired in heavy silk gown, and every hair on his head in the right place. Princess Beatrice played the Harmonium very well. The Queen has the Hymns written out very large for her, and then uses a magnifying glass.

The Empress Eugénie with the Duchesse de Berwick et d' Albe[1] and her [the Duchesse's] brother the Marquis de la Mina dined here. We received them in the hall, and the Princesses were so kind as I passed, and made me put on a fichu because of the open door. But the Empress went into the drawing-room and the Duchesse d' Albe came with us to the billiard-room, but it was only a minute. I felt so interested to watch the Empress and Queen together at dinner, the Empress with still traces of beauty and much grace and graciousness.[2] She walked first before the Queen and sat on her right. The Empress came up and spoke to me in French directly after dinner, and I asked after Comtesse Pourtalès and the Duchesse de Mouchy which prolonged the talk. The Empress spoke to Dr Story after he left the Queen and he was pleased as he had not been presented. The Queen's Indian servant, Mustafa, did not come quite in time and the Queen was quite fussed to accompany the Empress to the hall. "Ma chère sœur," as I heard the Queen call her as they went in to dinner. Plum pudding is served before the Roti on Sunday, a custom since the time of George IV I was told. [This custom is no longer followed.]

[1] The Empress's niece by marriage (her only sister had married the Duke of Alba), mother of the 17th Duke who was Spanish Ambassador in London from 1939 to 1945.

[2] Lady Lytton must have heard the gossip that Lord Clarendon was the Empress's father, and would therefore be particularly interested in watching her, for she might be her first cousin.

Monday, October 7

A quiet day. Drove in the afternoon to Glenmuick and saw Alice Borthwick upstairs as she had had a fall from her tricycle upsetting, wrist much swollen. Very fussed at the Peerage not being arranged.[1] The Queen asked me in the evening to write to Lord Salisbury about it, which I did of course, though I feel he has good reasons for delay. Evening easy.

Tuesday, October 8

Walked in the morning, after Alick Yorke had been to greet me.[2] Lovely day, such warm sun and lovely lights. Fräulein Colomb, Sir Matthew W. Ridley, Baron Hahn and Alick Yorke on the box went with me to Braemar, and we had tea at the Inn. The Queen with four horses drove through the town while we were standing there. Braemar is supposed to be a most bracing place, and I felt the air to be very fine. Very nice quiet evening watching the Princesses over their patiences.

Wednesday, October 9

Awful east wind and rain all day. We all went at three to a young Albert Brown's funeral, nephew of John Brown.[3]

Miss Phipps and I were in a close Brougham and the Queen and Princesses in a shut Landau which was drawn up at the door of the house where the coffin was brought out, and covered with a *plaid*. The minister from Ballater read some sentences out of our burial service and then gave a fine extempore prayer. It was most touching to see the Queen's carriage, with her taking part there, and it is the custom in Scotland and Germany, Princess Christian told me, for the Landlord always to follow any of his people to the

---

[1] Alice Borthwick was Lady Lytton's first cousin. Her husband, Sir Algernon Borthwick, was proprietor of the *Morning Post*. Each autumn the Borthwicks rented Glenmuick, the house adjoining Birkhall, belonging to Sir Allan Mackenzie. Sir Algernon had been promised a peerage.

[2] Alick Yorke was a Groom-in-Waiting and another of Lady Lytton's first cousins.

[3] He was the son of William Brown, a younger brother of John Brown, a farmer who had lived all his life in the neighbourhood of Balmoral. The Queen had attended Albert's christening on 1 November 1868.

grave. The Queen followed the hearse (an awful carriage with plumes, which the Queen declared after, when we were driving, should never be used again, and she would have a plain one got) to the entrance of a narrow lane, to the Churchyard, and then drove back to the poor mother's house, and sat for half an hour with her, weeping with, and helping her, not minding any inconvenience to herself. The Princesses went in another carriage, and Miss Phipps and I waited for the Queen. I was dreading the open carriage with such wind and rain, but luckily the Queen kept it shut. She spoke much of the young man who was just starting as a doctor, and the resignation of the mother: "They always are so resigned these good people." The house which had been built for John Brown was full of Royal prints and presents. The father kept himself up with whiskey and had to be supported by two at the ceremony, so Mrs Brown was right that the Queen had better see him another day. The Queen called at three cottages, had the women out and gave them stuff for dresses so kindly. She had a nap at the end but Miss Phipps roused her before we got home.

Mustafa must be very strong as he stood in the drenching rain at the funeral.

Lady Clanwilliam[1] and Bessy Meade [her daughter] dined, but the evening without cards was dull, but the Queen spoke to all.

I received a kind telegram from Lord Salisbury, "Your letter just received. I am addressing myself immediately to the matter to which you refer,"[2] and I told the Queen. Princess Christian was so kind and cheering about my doing all right and declared, "Mama is very pleased."

Thursday, October 10

Only walking with bad bitterly cold weather, but I feel much stronger and am getting quite fat.

Enjoyed the dinner between Slatin Pasha and Major

[1] Lord and Lady Clanwilliam with their daughter were staying at Birkhall. The 4th Earl of Clanwilliam was an Admiral of the Fleet and had been Queen Victoria's Naval A.D.C.

[2] So immediately did Lord Salisbury address himself to the matter that Sir Algernon Borthwick was created Baron Glenesk on October 12.

Wingate who organised the Pasha's escape after twelve
years captivity in the Sudan. He is a gentle looking brown
Eastern (aged thirty-eight looking forty or more) though
born an Austrian. The Queen had decorated him with the
C.B. which gave him great pleasure of course and he is to be
employed in the Intelligence Department at Cairo. He was
rescued last February through spies and traders, and at the
last just a whisper came to him from a donkey boy to get on
the donkey after the Service, at the Mosque, of which he
attended five daily. A dust storm helped him to escape
and he only rode out of the town, and then with guides,
who had been organised and paid, got away with camels,
but constantly had to hide in mountains and with hardly
anything to eat. One day he was just roasting a sheep whole,
and three hundred troops were coming so Slatin fled and
the troops ate up his meal.

The Khalifa who succeeded the Mahdi had four hundred
wives and when tired of one used to give her away or offer
her to Slatin. What a contrast now is the time when Slatin
was running as a slave by the Khalifa's horse. He chose a
very sharp sword on reaching Cairo, and hopes to run it into
the Khalifa, should he ever return to the Sudan.

[Rudolf Carl Slatin was born in 1857 of a well known
Viennese family. He became a professional soldier, and in
1878, when serving as a first lieutenant in the Crown
Prince Rudolf's regiment, received a letter from General
Gordon inviting him to come to the Sudan to take service
with the Egyptian Government under his direction. He had
previously, in 1874, undertaken a journey to the Sudan and
had there made contact with General Gordon who was at
the time Governor-General of the Equatorial Provinces.
He accepted Gordon's offer out of a sense of adventure and
was first made financial inspector, and then, in 1881,
appointed Governor-General of Darfur. Two years later he
became nominally a Moslem, believing that it was the
only way to hold the loyalty of his troops against the rise of
the Mahdi. In December 1883 he was forced to surrender
to the Mahdi, and was held prisoner by him and his successor,

the Khalifa, until February 1895 when he escaped to Cairo.

In 1896 he published an account of his experiences under the title *Fire and Sword in the Soudan*, translated and edited by his great friend Reginald Wingate, and dedicated to the Queen. It had an immense success, and is still fascinating and exciting reading. Wingate was able to avenge Slatin for he was in command of the British forces which destroyed the Khalifa in 1899.

In August 1895 Slatin and Wingate had been to Osborne and the Queen had written in her journal on August 19: "Slatin Pasha, who had escaped from his long captivity with the Mahdi, three months ago, and Major Wingate who had been instrumental in his escape, arrived. After dinner I decorated Major Wingate with the C.B. Had a great deal of conversation with him and Slatin Pasha, which was most interesting. The latter is a charming modest little man, whom no one could think had gone through such vicissitudes, for he looks so well; but there are lines in his face which betoken mental suffering. His final escape was quite miraculous. He had been eleven years in captivity and nine months in irons. While he was in prison, they brought him General Gordon's head to look at. Slatin Pasha gave me a small printed account of his escape. Major Wingate is a very clever, distinguished officer and his great friend. They generally speak Arabic together, as Slatin knows no English and very little French,[1] whilst Major Wingate cannot speak German. Slatin is Austrian by birth. What has been a great sorrow to him, is that his mother died before hearing of his escape."

On September 30 of the same year Sir Arthur Bigge wrote to the Queen (though he was with her at Balmoral):

"Sir Arthur Bigge humbly begs to submit to your Majesty. Lord Wolseley has forwarded to him a letter from Major Wingate, who raises the question of the advisability of Slatin Pasha's receiving some English decoration or

---

[1] It is stated in *Wingate of the Sudan* by Sir Ronald Wingate, who knew Slatin personally, that "he spoke French and English as well as he spoke his mother tongue German."

medal. After Slatin's return to Cairo the Khedive tried hard to secure him for his Household in a civilian capacity, and to remove him from contact with British officers. This Slatin refused to do, preferring to resign the Egyptian service unless allowed to serve in the Army. After considerable opposition Lord Cromer [Consul-General in Egypt] got him appointed to the Intelligence Department. He has acted most loyally in British interests, openly protesting against French intrigues; and consequently has incurred some Khedival disfavour. Probably on this account the Khedive has abstained from giving him any decoration or medal.[1] Slatin has felt this considerably; as for four years, as Governor of Darfur, he struggled most loyally to uphold Egyptian authority in that province. His long imprisonment was the result of the Gordon relief expedition.[2] During his captivity he managed occasionally to supply us with very valuable information at great personal risk, and his future services will of course be invaluable to us. . . . Sir Arthur humbly submits whether your Majesty would approve of Lord Salisbury being asked whether Slatin might not receive the C.M.G. and the Egyptian medal. . . . He is not a British subject. But Colonel V. Knesebeck[3] was given the Military C.B."

Lord Salisbury approved and Slatin received the Civil C.B. When the Queen decorated him she noted in her journal for October 11 that he was "ready at any time to shed his blood in my service." In 1900 he was made Inspector General of the Sudan, a post specially created for him which he held until 1914. He was knighted in 1898 and created a Baron of the Austrian Empire in 1906. He died in 1932.

Wilfred Blunt, the poet, had a very poor opinion of Slatin. He met him at the War Office on 3 February 1895 and wrote in his *Diaries*: "I had some talk with Slatin, a commonplace little German, quite unworthy of ever having served the Mahdi." And on 24 October 1896 he wrote: "I have

---

[1] The Khedive did, however, make him a Pasha.

[2] His capture had in fact nothing to do with the Gordon Relief Expedition. He surrendered to the Madhi in December 1883, whereas Gordon did not arrive in the Sudan until February 1884.

[3] The Colonel of the Queen's German regiment.

been reading Slatin's *Fire and Sword in the Soudan*, a sensational volume written with a purpose, the style obviously Wingate's, as it is identical to his 'Ohrwalder' book.[1] Slatin is a mean wretch to have published it, and the Mahdi made a mistake in not cutting his head off at once when he surrendered, and sending him straight to Paradise. His professions of loyalty to the Khedive and to our gracious Queen are fulsome, and those of disloyalty to the people whose religion he adopted to save his miserable life, disgusting."]

October 11

Horrid cold wind and misty rain in the afternoon, only took walks, one round the hill in the afternoon with the Germans and Slatin. After tea Slatin and Major Wingate showed us how Slatin had to sit on the ground with his eyes down and arms crossed before the Khalifa and it was very interesting.

The Empress Eugénie and Madame Délices dined here. But the evening was rather stiff, and so much standing. I had a little talk with the Empress between getting people for the Queen to talk with.

October 12

Lovely quite warm day. Walked to see the Church which is very good plain building and stands out well. Drove Slatin and Major Wingate to the forest and mountain. He told us an old Arab had once recommended him, "to be patient and cheerful, and said if he lived long he would see much." And this had been a constant help in his difficulties.[2]

[1] Father Ohrwalder, a member of the Austrian Roman Catholic Mission in the Sudan, had been captured by the Madhi in 1882, and had escaped with Wingate's help in December 1891. Wingate persuaded the Father to write his experiences, which he translated and re-wrote under the title of *Ten Years Captivity in the Madhi's Camp*. The book had a tremendous success when it was published in 1892.

[2] It was Slatin's old enemy, Madibbo, Chief of the Rizighat tribe and an adherent of the Mahdi, who said to Slatin when he was in captivity: "Be obedient and patient (God is with the patient), for he who lives long sees much." These words obviously made a great impression on Slatin for he quotes them several times in his book *Fire and Sword in the Soudan*. He finished the book that October, 1895.

3

Sunday, October 13

Blowy and chilly but no rain. Went to the Service in the Church. Great fuss about arrangements as only announced in the morning. I went in the second carriage with Princess Beatrice and Princess Victoria after the Queen's carriage. The Church Service was very well done and the hymns good and I am sure the Queen went to please her people, and especially those in sorrow, and she looked out for them with her double glasses as she is now very blind, and glasses don't help her much.

The Queen said she was afraid the wind would ruffle her hair getting into her carriage, so she cared to look well.

There were pretty hymns and "Peace, Perfect Peace" amongst them, and a fairly good preacher from near Edinburgh, Mr Fleming.[1] I felt pains in my limbs and shivers and dreaded having to leave in the evening, if I got worse, but luckily I got better, but felt very stupid myself, but sat by Fritz Ponsonby[2] who chats very easily. The evening was very solemn though the Queen enjoys talking then, but after eleven all the other Princesses get fidgety and Miss Phipps is often told by Princess Beatrice to interrupt the Queen and remind her it is past eleven, which is very difficult of course.

Monday, October 14

Lovely day and so sunny, and fresh. Last nice walk with Fräulein Colomb who has been always so nice and been out with me twice a day. Went to the hall to see Princess Christian, Princess Victoria and Prince and Princess Henry of Prussia and their dear little Prince Waldemar [he was six years old], with such pretty manners, off at three. Dear Princess Christian so cordial always, said she would visit me at the Danes. I am afraid she could not get in and out!

[1] Dr Archibald Fleming afterwards became Minister of St Columba's, Pont St.

[2] Frederick (1867–1935), the second son of Sir Henry Ponsonby. Made an Equerry in 1894, he was to remain at Court for more than forty years. In 1935 he was created Baron Sysonby. He was responsible for the publication of the Empress Frederick's letters to Queen Victoria. In 1899 he married Victoria (Ria), daughter of Colonel Kennard, the Queen having made him wait three years. In the end it was Miss Phipps who persuaded her to give her consent, but it was with the understanding that he should never be given a house in the Queen's lifetime.

Miss Phipps and I had to receive the Empress Eugénie at four and she drove with the Queen. Then we drove a little, and went to the shop [Mrs. Symons's shop. See p. 119] to meet Lady Biddulph, Freda and Gerry Liddell.[1]. She had had a dreadful sixteen hours passage from Dublin to Glasgow with heavy seas and sickness but was very calm over it.

Delightful quiet small dinner, only the three ladies, with Miss Majendie [Maid-of-Honour] who had arrived, making six with the Queen and Prince and Princess Henry of Battenberg, and conversation general and so easy and the evening also.

The Queen told me she remembered Lady Normanby [Lady Lytton's aunt] telling her my father and mother were just married looking like two pale asparagus, so pale and very poor, and that was in 1835.

Tuesday, October 15

Great talking in the morning about who was going to the ceremony of the stone-laying of the new house at Mar Lodge.[2] Miss Phipps kindly helped me over the dress question. Alick and I drove in front in a close carriage, ready to receive the Queen and Prince and Princess. The road and birch trees all yellow, looked lovely. The Queen has a coachman who used till last year to drive the Dorking Coach and he is very clever without ever using his whip, and the outriders on greys and then the four grey horses looked so well as they arrived. Miss Forbes[3] received us, then we saw

[1] Geraldine Liddell, yet another of Lady Lytton's first cousins. Lady Biddulph was a Lady-in-Waiting to Princess Beatrice and the widow of Sir Thomas Biddulph, Keeper of the Privy Purse. Freda was her daughter. They were all staying at Birkhall.

[2] Belonging to the Duke of Fife, twelve miles from Balmoral. The Duchess of Fife was Princess Louise, the eldest daughter of the Prince of Wales. New Mar Lodge, or Curriemulzie as it was originally called, had been burnt down earlier in the year due to the carelessness of a plumber who had left a lighted candle under the floor. The new house took three years to build. It was not on the site of the old one, but on the other side of the river, close to Old Mar Lodge where the Fifes lived while it was being built. The new house was to have a hundred and twenty rooms and was partly designed by the Duchess herself.

[3] Miss Forbes was either Blanche, daughter of Sir Charles Forbes of Newe, or her cousin Ida, daughter of George Stewart Forbes, both of whom were great friends of the Duchess of Fife and frequently went to Mar Lodge. Blanche married in 1903 John Blundell Leigh, and Ida married on 30 November

the Duke and Duchess of Fife in the hall when the Queen was coming. Her Majesty went to a bedroom prepared for her to put on her *cap*, then we lunched. The Duke of Fife kept up talk very well, talk not of a very high type. The Duchess so nice in manners but did not talk much. The little ladies Fife came down muffled in shawls and are delicate but such little dears.[1] The *many* dishes were well prepared. The Queen then retired to put on a bonnet, and was rather long, but I at last suggested to the Duchess to tell her all was ready. The Queen went in her chair, the Duke of Fife holding an umbrella for it was raining. Princess Beatrice had my shower dust cloak to cover her crape. The Pipers piping, and the Fife men with spears and kilts looked well, and gave hearty cheers, and the Queen seemed very pleased. I stood close behind her but fear the photos will not come out well.

Then all returned to the House, and the Clanwilliams, Mr Leslie, the factor, and the Clergyman came to be presented, and the Queen looked at the plans. Tea was served for the people who had been standing in the tent. The Queen went a third time to her room, to put on her hat and left soon after four. I drove back with the Queen and Princess but the hood was soon put up my side so I was well protected. The talk was about the Ceremony, the little children; "They ought to go to the South for the winter and live out of doors." We stopped at a cottage to see a stout "Maggie." "Have you got any money?" said the Queen to the Scotch servant, a stout man who can't move without being so blown he can't speak. "Aboot twelve shillings." "Ah, that won't do *at all*, I always give her five poond," answered the Queen with the Scotch accent.

Princess Beatrice bore the umbrella hitting her cheek *so* well and is so quiet with the Queen. Lord James [of Hereford, Chancellor of the Duchy of Lancaster] came and was at dinner showing great signs of his recent illness. [He suffered very badly from gout.] We stood and drank the health of the

1895, Sir Archibald Edmonstone. Sir Charles Forbes and his brother George had founded the East India House of Forbes, Forbes and Co. and were the oldest of the Prince of Wales's financial advisers among his friends.
    [1] Alexandra and Maud Duff were four and two.

Duke of Coburg's son who attained his majority.[1] Evening very solemn and room so cold.

Wednesday, October 16

Fine day but cold. Walked with Miss Majendie, a nice girl but rather shy. Seems great friends with everyone of the household. Marie Mallet arrived early very tired and rather alarmed also, because till one knows what is expected of one, one cannot be at one's ease, but the Queen likes the change of new people I told her, and tried to cheer her.[2] Princess Beatrice is also very fond of Marie. Lord James, Alick (Yorke), Miss Majendie and I drove to Birkhall to see Lady Biddulph and Gerry [Liddell]. Lord James talked with wonderful ease and brilliancy both ways, a good deal about actors, and then political people. He thinks Asquith very clever and that he could do anything he likes but with his want of sympathy, he will never get others to work with him. He thinks him so hard. He remembered Harcourt saying at the time of the marriage, how he pitied his wife as he thought she would be miserable in two years but it does not seem to be so.[3] Then stories of Lord Russell, Disraeli etc. were all most pleasant.

Our dinner of seven, and evening were the most perfect we have had. The Queen said on sitting down to dinner to Prince Henry [of Battenberg], "I *a* do*a*nt know why the candles give no*a* light now, it is so *daark.*" It was rather pathetic. He passed it off and I don't know whether it struck him the eyes are getting so dim. Small talk was animated at dinner. There was Quenelles à la Lytton in the menu,

[1] The Duke of Coburg was Queen Victoria's second son Alfred, formerly Duke of Edinburgh. He had inherited the Duchy of Saxe-Coburg and Gotha, on the death in 1893 of the Prince Consort's brother, Ernest. His only son, Alfred, was brought up in Germany and died in 1899 after a riotous youth.

[2] Marie Mallet was the Hon. Mrs Bernard Mallet, Lady Lytton's first cousin once removed. Before her marriage, as Marie Adeane, she had been a Maid-of-Honour but had only recently been appointed a Woman-of-the-Bedchamber.

[3] Herbert Asquith's first wife, Helen, elder daughter of Dr Frederick Melland, whom he had married in 1877, had died in 1891, and in 1894 he had married Margot Tennant after a long courtship. Asquith was Home Secretary in Gladstone's Cabinet at the time Sir William Harcourt was said to have made these remarks about him.

Prince Henry said would please me. Soon after we went into the drawing-room, Herr Wolff [violinist] was sent for and played to Princess Beatrice's accompaniment. (Rather weak but following so well, good time, no wrong notes and very soft.) The Queen made me sit by her, and she looked radiant and enjoyed it so much and talked over each piece, and Wolff seemed in an ecstasy and said looking at the Queen inspired him! The Queen also praised the pieces and kept talking over them just as an artist would like. Wolff said Grieg was not appreciated in Germany. "What fools," said the Queen, when it was suggested individuals might like him but not the general audience. It seemed to us ladies the most perfect luxury to enjoy it all so quietly.

October 17

A white frost, seven degrees, and the loveliest clearest day I ever saw. It reminded me of the hills in India in October. Emily Ampthill came at twelve and stayed an hour and I went a little way with her and walked home.[1] It was so nice having a talk. Drive with the Queen. Her Majesty spoke of the Munshi for the first time and wished me to see him and his wife as "he was presented to Lord Lytton at Gratz."[2] My one and only wish is to please the Queen. Then she said the Armenians were also to blame in the late row, and she wished the Mahommedans could be let alone by Missionaries, and many things in which I agree, but rather implying she discussed them with the Munshi which is a risk.

[The Munshi, Abdul Karim, is one of the most fascinating figures of the last years of Victoria's reign. A Mahommedan, he had been brought to Balmoral in 1887, four years after the death of John Brown, with some other Indian khitmutgars to wait on the Queen, and his duties at first seem to have been confined to handing round dishes and standing behind

---

[1] The Dowager Lady Ampthill, Lady Lytton's first cousin, was a Lady-in-Waiting. She was staying at Glenmuick with the Glenesks, and went into waiting at Balmoral when Lady Lytton left on the 19th.

[2] Lady Lytton must have meant Grasse, where Lord Lytton went to see the Queen the year before his death. He never went to Austria after the Munshi's arrival in England.

THE QUEEN WITH THE MUNSHI

the Queen while she was signing documents, to dry her signature. She found that he learnt with "extraordinary assiduity" and was "a great comfort" to her.

He was soon relieved of all domestic duties, for he maintained that he did not belong to the servant class and that his father was a Surgeon-General in the Indian Army at Agra. His salary was increased and all photographs of him handing dishes to the Queen were destroyed. Moreover he was told by the Queen to join the Household in the billiard-room, a privilege to which the rest of the courtiers strongly objected, and Sir Henry Ponsonby had the greatest difficulty in getting them to so much as say good-morning to him. He was promoted to being the Queen's Munshi (*munshi* simply means teacher in Urdu and Hindustani), went everywhere with her and gave her daily lessons in Hindustani. It was very laudable that she should have tried to learn Hindustani, for the lessons must have been very difficult to fit into her tightly-packed routine. Her reward came when she was able to speak a few words of the language to the Indian soldiers who came over to England for her Diamond Jubilee in 1897.

Naturally her favouritism aroused jealousy, and the Munshi seems to have been as much disliked by her family and Household as John Brown had been, and no one would have disliked him more, one feels, than John Brown himself. It is difficult to imagine a greater contrast than between these two strange favourites, but whereas his worst enemy could not have accused John Brown of disloyalty, the Munshi was suspected of being a spy. The Queen, who trusted him absolutely, showed him secret dispatches from India and there were said to be leakages through the contacts he had in India. In 1894 attacks on him began to appear in the newspapers, and his claim to be the son of a surgeon, as well as his loyalty, was questioned.

The Queen wrote indignantly to Sir Henry Ponsonby from Florence on 10 April 1894 about "the stupid illnatured article or rather letter about the poor good Munshi and she would wish to observe that to make out that he is so *low* is really *outrageous* and in a country like England quite out of place. . . . She has known two Archbishops who were the sons respectively of a Butcher and a Grocer, a Chancellor whose father was a poor sort of Scotch Minister, Sir D. Stewart and Lord Mount Stephen both who ran about barefoot as children and whose parents were very humble. . . . Abdul's father saw good honourable service as a Dr and he [Abdul] feels cut to the heart at being thus spoken of. It probably comes from some low jealous Indians or Anglo-Indians. . . . The Queen is so sorry for the poor Munshi's sensitive feelings."[1]

When Frederick Ponsonby was appointed Equerry in 1894 he was still in India as A.D.C. to the Viceroy, Lord Elgin. This was just at the time when the Munshi's origin was being questioned and the Queen telegraphed to Ponsonby and asked him to go and see the Munshi's father, the Surgeon-General in Agra. Ponsonby duly went and discovered that he was not a Surgeon-General at all but the apothecary at the jail. When he returned to England and took up his appointment, the Queen at once asked him whether he had been to see the Munshi's father and he told her what he had discovered. The Queen refused to believe it and maintained that he must have seen the wrong man, but Ponsonby, not realising how much was involved, stuck to his assertion.[2] To show her displeasure the Queen did not speak a word to him for the next month, and she did not ask him to dine with her for the whole of the first year he was in her Household. Could it be that his first appearance at her dinner table was the evening of October 13 when Lady Lytton sat next to him and found that "he chats very easily"?

Lord George Hamilton, who became Secretary of State for India in 1895, at last managed to stop the Queen from showing the Munshi confidential papers by warning her that it would be impossible for him to go on sending them to *her* if she continued to do so, and also by pointing out that her Hindu subjects would very much resent a

---

[1] *Henry Ponsonby*, by Arthur Ponsonby.

[2] Lord Curzon, when Viceroy, was more tactful. He wrote to the Queen from Calcutta on 21 December 1899: "While at Agra the Viceroy had the pleasure of making the acquaintance of the father of your Majesty's Munshi. He was a courtly old gentleman, and had many interesting experiences to relate."

Mahommedan being given a position of so much power; but to show her own confidence in the Munshi she decorated him with the C.I.E. and appointed him her official Indian Secretary, Hafiz Abdul Karim, and as such he appeared thereafter in the Court Circular. Moreover a bungalow was built for him at Osborne and a house given to him at Balmoral, both fully furnished down to plate and linen. At Windsor he lived in Frogmore Cottage.

The Queen went on fighting his battles with undaunted staunchness, which only increased his unpopularity, and during this October, 1895, she was writing to Lord Salisbury to urge him to appoint Ahmed Rafiuddin, a friend of the Munshi who was reading for the bar in London, to a diplomatic post in Constantinople. Though the Munshi greatly fostered her natural interest in India, he seems to have given her a bias in favour of Mahommedans. Even over the question of Turkish atrocities against the Armenians she could not bear to be thought unjust to the Moslems, "of whom I have more subjects than the Sultan" she proudly wrote to Lord Salisbury on 23 October 1895.

Mr Pope-Hennessy in his life of Queen Mary writes: "The Queen's Household loathed the Munshi: 'The Indian servants behind her chair looked rather splendid,' a surviving member of Queen Victoria's Household recently remarked, 'we could take them, but the Munshi was so personally repulsive and disagreeable that he was impossible. He made endless trouble too.' " On her last visit to France in 1899 "the Queen had been determined to take the Munshi with her," Mr Pope-Hennessy goes on. "This would have involved him eating with the ladies and gentlemen of the Household, 'who put their feet down at this and refused.' The Queen's personal secretary, Miss Harriet Phipps, remonstrated with the Queen, who became so incensed that she swept all the objects off her writing-table on to the floor. The Household then prepared to go on strike or to resign in a body. The Prime Minister, Lord Salisbury, who was coming down to Windsor, was appealed to by the Household. He told the Queen that the French were 'such odd people' they might laugh at Her Majesty about the

Munshi. This had momentarily the desired effect. The Munshi was left behind, but not for long. 'Gdmama again spoke about the M——i who to the despair of the poor gentlemen arrived today,' Princess May wrote to her husband [the Duke of York] from Cimiez on 1 April. 'I was most guarded in my replies.' "

Though one can understand that the Munshi was disliked, as favourites nearly always are, it is difficult to believe that he was "so personally repulsive", for Queen Victoria was as sensitive as any woman to male attraction. One cannot help feeling that the repugnance with which he was regarded by the Household was based mostly on snobbery and colour prejudice. There were few English people in those days who would sit down at table with an Indian were he not a prince. The Queen—herself blessedly free from colour prejudice— must indeed have felt exasperated by the attitude of her Household.]

We drove to Ballater and back by the Hill road and at the cross-roads which lead to Glenmuick and Birkhall, we waited and Mustafa, the Indian servant, and a Scotchman were preparing tea which was brought to the carriage. It was a chilly place but rather fun. We got home by six and it was cold by then. The dinner and evening were rather solemn and dull.

October 18

White frost early but lovely day and clear. In the afternoon Miss Majendie and I drove with the Queen, who was rather tired and sleepy but we managed to wake her by changing her cloak and talking when it seemed better to do so, but I thought she would be fresher in the evening for having a little sleep and it was so, for she never rests in her room I believe.

We had tea at the Donald Stewarts' Lodge and the good scones again, and Princess Beatrice joined us. The Queen said she heard Sir Henry Ponsonby had had a cough and spoke with great feeling about them all, and when I said how terribly she must have missed him, she told me she had been rather prepared for it as Sir Henry was not well at Balmoral last year, and his handwriting changed a good deal. She feels most tenderly with Lady Ponsonby.

I drove home alone with the Queen and she spoke of the ceremony at Wörth of unveiling the Emperor Frederick's Statue would be trying for her daughter the Empress.[1] Then she alluded to the Emperor [William II] having behaved so badly to his mother, but it was better now. I said the Emperor was devoted to the Queen and I was sure she had helped him. "Oh, not much and I *never interfere* in politics." I said I thought she had much helped the Princess of Wales also but the Queen said, "She will not be *advised* as is common with *young* people."

We had many artists quietly in the drawing-room after dinner, Wolff, Albani, Hollman, Clara Butt, Salmond and Pugno. Only the Biddulphs and Gerry Liddell came in the evening, but the Dean of Windsor and Mrs Eliot dined. I sat by the Queen and her manner to the radiant artists was perfect, and they were so happy and each did extra well. Gounod's *Ave Maria* with Wolff and Albani was perfect. Albani received a *sapphire* bracelet and Miss Butt the decoration which Albani has which I gave from the Queen, and the gentlemen will each receive something and all their expenses *paid*. The household supped with the artists and guests and it was very merry.[2]

The statue was unveiled on the 18th. On 6 August 1870 the Germans, under the command of Frederick, then Crown Prince, had won a great victory against the French at Wörth. Thereafter Frederick was known as the Victor of Wörth. He died in 1888 after reigning for only ninety-nine days. The unveiling was indeed trying for the widowed Empress. She wrote next day to her daughter Sophie, "What I felt I cannot describe, all my loneliness seemed to come upon me at once."

[2] Madame Albani was on a concert tour of England and Scotland with the artists who went with her to Balmoral. (See Biographical Index.) Since 1883 she had spent a holiday nearly every autumn at Old Mar Lodge, with the Fifes, and would go each time to sing to the Queen. She first sang before the Queen at Windsor in 1874. The decoration given to Clara Butt, who was then twenty-two, must have been the Golden Jubilee Medal, for that was the only British decoration Albani possessed. It was given to her by the Queen at Balmoral on 5 October 1887. In 1925 she was created Dame of the Order of the British Empire, founded in 1917.

Saturday, October 19

The most lovely clear day and warmer. The Queen wished me to go to see Mrs Karim and the Munshi at their house so Miss Phipps came with me. She is a nice little woman and had such a pretty native dress and jewels. He came in very jauntily after a bit and put out his hand *à l'Anglaise*, so of course we took it, but he did not sit down and we did not stay long. I wrote my name in his book where many Royalties have written. I wonder what he writes home to his country? The Queen now calls him her Indian Secretary and I am afraid he will not understand being so spoilt. (The Munshi was sent back to India directly the Queen died and his house and papers all went for fear he had copies of dispatches.)[1]

The Queen said good-bye to me on coming in from her pony chair, in the passage and hoped I should find all the family well, and I went to Princess Beatrice's room to make my bow to her. Miss Phipps and I left together at 2.15 and I came home by the night train from Aberdeen very comfortably in the Pullman car, only one sees nothing. Got back to the Danes by eleven. Con met me at Cole Green and has prepared so many flowers in the rooms and given me such a hearty welcome, God Bless her, and my Ems comes back to-morrow.

Nice letter from dear Vic to say he has passed all his "little go" exam at Cambridge and hopes he has done with mathematics which he hates.

---

[1] This was a later note in Lady Lytton's handwriting. When King Edward VII came to the throne he got rid of all his mother's Indian servants and burnt the Munshi's papers.

Chapter Two

LADY LYTTON was next in waiting at Osborne in the following February. Osborne House was built, and the gardens laid out, by Prince Albert himself with the help of Thomas Cubitt, the London builder, between 1845 and 1851. It is on the site of an old house which the Queen had bought in 1845 with an estate of a thousand acres. It has a wonderful sea view and a private beach which cannot be seen from any public place. After the Prince Consort's death it was to Osborne that the Queen retired in her misery, for it was there, in their joint creation, that her memories of him were most acute.

In 1904 King Edward, who had no use for Osborne, made over most of the estate to the nation, but only the state apartments in the house were opened to the public. In 1954, however, the present Queen granted permission for the private suites also to be shown to the public on certain week-days, and it is in these that the fascination of the house lies. The dressing-rooms with their old fashioned baths and showers; the Queen's mahogany-encased lavatory; her bedroom with the miniature of her husband pinned to the bedhead on his side of the bed just as it was when she first became a widow; the double desk in her sitting-room with the ivory bell-pulls where she and Albert worked side by side, and Albert's own sitting-room with his walking sticks and umbrellas still in the rack and all his personal belongings lying around, unchanged from the day he died—it all has such poignancy that one comes away so drenched in old emotion that it is as if one had undergone a startling personal experience of reincarnation. The only change is that now the rooms smell dead whereas Queen Marie of Roumania tells us that the Queen's rooms, wherever she was, smelt of orange flower even when no flowers were there. Was this smell of orange flower always surrounding the Queen part of her attraction?

When Lady Lytton arrived at Osborne in February 1896 the Court was in deep mourning for the Queen's beloved son-in-law, Prince Henry of Battenberg. Only three weeks before he had died of fever on his way home from the Ashanti expedition. He had never been popular in England with the public at large, but that was forgotten now in the intense wave of sympathy for the Queen and Princess Beatrice, the best known of all the Princesses, which swept the country.

There had been great disappointment in the country when, in 1885, Beatrice married Prince Henry, for it had been hoped that she would marry an Englishman like her sister, Louise, who four years before had married the Marquess of Lorne, the heir to the Duke of Argyll; and the Prince's unpopularity grew when it was found that unlike his brother, Prince Louis, who was an Admiral of the Fleet, and his brother-in-law, Prince Christian, who was a General in the British Army, he was not to serve his adopted country. He was made Governor of the Isle of Wight and of Carisbrooke Castle, but these posts, although he took them as seriously as he could, were no more than sinecures. Poor young man (he was only twenty-seven when he married), he must have been dreadfully irked by the narrowness and inactivity of his life, and deeply wounded by the lampoons on him which appeared in the press. Sir Henry Ponsonby wrote to his wife from Balmoral in November 1887: "One of the Society papers—the low ones—gives a sketch of Prince Henry's life here and says he tries to get through the day by playing billiards with Sir Henry Ponsonby, 'no mean wielder of the cue—but an astute courtier who never permits himself to beat his opponent.' I never saw Prince Henry playing billiards at all." One malicious cartoon showed him lounging in a velvet jacket, smoking a long German pipe.

But Liko, as he was called in the family, was dearly loved at Court, except perhaps by the Prince of Wales who was rather jealous of his intimacy with the Queen. He was full of fun and an excellent shot and horseman. As well as sweetening the Queen's life and making Princess Beatrice a very happy

woman, he had endeared himself to the ladies of the Household by his gaiety and charming manners, and to the gentlemen by persuading the Queen to relax her rule of allowing
smoking at Balmoral only in a tiny room with a bare
wooden table and chair in it which must be reached by
crossing the open kitchen yard and which the Queen looked
upon as a kind of opium den. Under Prince Henry's influence
a larger room, which, though still near the servants' quarters,
was accessible without going out of doors and furnished with
armchairs, sofas and writing-tables, was given over to the
smokers. Another such room was provided at Osborne, while
at Windsor smoking was permitted in the billiard-room.
Prince Henry gave up smoking for a time when the Duke of
Edinburgh took possession of the smoking room and talked
about himself by the hour. From all accounts the Duke seems
to have been a great bore, as well as an excruciatingly bad
violin player, and there was general rejoicing at Court when
in 1893 he inherited the Duchy of Coburg and went to live
there.

It was a wonder that Princess Beatrice ever married. She
had been four years old when her father died, and since then
had been continually with her mother, and it seems doubtful
whether the Queen would have allowed her to marry if she
had not found a husband who was willing to live with his
mother-in-law; and the Queen might not have accepted even
a resident son-in-law if John Brown had still been alive,
but Brown had died in the spring of 1883, and she grievously
missed the daily companionship of a reliable man.

After the death of Princess Alice in 1878, the Queen had
conceived the wild idea of marrying Beatrice to the widower,
the Grand Duke of Hesse, so that she might become step-
mother to Alice's four children, with the understanding, of
course, that she and the children should spend most of their
time with her in England. This preposterous plan was illegal
among other things, but with the extra determination she
showed whenever she was baulked, the Queen hoped to get a
bill passed through Parliament altering the law. Five months
after Princess Alice's death, on 7 May 1879, she wrote in her
journal: "Saw Lord Beaconsfield at 1. Talked of the loss of

the Bill, permitting the marriage with a sister-in-law, in favour of which Bertie presented a petition, and which we are most anxious should pass. It has passed the Commons but is thrown out in the Lords, the Bishops being so much against it. Lord Beaconsfield is in favour of it, but the whole Cabinet against it! Incredible!"[1]

One does not know what Princess Beatrice herself thought of this plan or whether she was ever told about it, but at this time she seems to have been much attached to the Prince Imperial, and the Empress Eugénie was certainly very anxious that they should marry. This romance was cut short, however, when the Prince was killed by the Zulus on 1 June 1879.

Princess Beatrice was twenty-five in 1884 when she went in April with the Queen to Darmstadt for the wedding of Prince Louis of Battenberg to Princess Victoria of Hesse (who, if the Queen had had her way, might have been her step-daughter) and there she met Prince Louis's younger brother, Henry, said to be the best looking of this handsome family, an officer in the Prussian Household Cavalry, whom she had not seen since she was a child. They fell in love and were married in July of the following year, not without family criticism, though, especially from Beatrice's nephew, Prince William of Prussia (the Kaiser to be) who was very contemptuous of the Battenberg stock and the newly-created title. But Queen Victoria put her grandson magnificently in his place in a letter to his mother, the Crown Princess Frederick: "If the Queen of England thinks a person good enough for her daughter what have other people got to say?"

They were married at the Osborne parish church at Whippingham, the first Royal wedding ever to take place in a parish church, and the guests found it difficult to know what to wear until a ruling was sent to the Lord Chamberlain for circulation, laying down that ladies staying in the Isle of Wight were "to wear long dresses with demi-toilette bodies, cut down at the back and with sleeves to the elbow, jewels to be worn on the dress and in the hair as for full dress

[1]The Deceased Wife's Sister Marriage Act was not passed until 1907.

evening party. Only those ladies who travel down to
Osborne for the day are to wear bonnets and smart morning
dresses."

Prince Henry wore at his wedding the white uniform of the
Gardes du Corps, which inspired the Princess of Wales to
call him "Beatrice's Lohengrin." The Queen wrote in her
journal: "Though I stood for the ninth time near a child
and the fifth time near a daughter, at the altar, I think I never
felt more deeply than I did on this occasion."

But even on her honeymoon Princess Beatrice, as she
continued to be called, was away for only two days from her
mother, and then she went no further than to a villa at Ryde.
On her marriage she received from Parliament a dowry of
£30,000 and an annuity of £6000. (The same settlement
was made on all Queen Victoria's daughters except the
Princess Royal who received a dowry of £40,000 and an
annuity of £8000. The Prince of Wales had the estates of
the Duchy of Cornwall, enormously increased in value under
the Prince Consort's management, and Sandringham as a
Dowry, and an income of £100,000, with a separate income
of £10,000 for the Princess of Wales; while dowries of
£30,000 and annuities of £15,000 were settled on the
younger sons.)

The marriage turned out to be a very happy one. Four
children were born to them in five years, Alexander, Ena,
Leopold and Maurice, and the Queen's contentment grew and
grew. There was only one shadow —Prince Henry was bored.
When in November 1895 King Prempeh of Kumasi ig-
nored the British Government's ultimatum to stop raiding
the Gold Coast for slaves, and it was decided to send out an
expedition to teach him a lesson, Prince Henry saw his
chance of escaping for a while from a woman's world and
volunteered for the post of Military Secretary to the Commander, Sir Francis Scott. At first the Queen said it "would
never do," but she was eventually persuaded to let him go by
Princess Beatrice herself.

On December 6, at Windsor, she wrote in her journal:
"Took tea with Beatrice and Liko, and directly afterwards he
came to wish me good-bye, and was much upset, knelt down

4

and kissed my hand and I embraced him. He said he went not
out of a sense of adventure but because he felt it was right. . . .
I could think of little else but this sad parting. God grant that
dear Liko may be brought back safe to us!"

But it was not to be. He arrived safely at Cape Coast,
having endeared himself to all on board by his high spirits,
and on December 27 started with the main column of the
Expeditionary Force to march towards Kumasi. On January
10, about forty miles from Kumasi, he went down with
malaria and the doctors insisted that he should be taken back
to Cape Coast. There, in spite of all his protests, he was
put on board H.M.S. *Blonde* which sailed immediately
for Madeira. On the evening of Monday, January 20,
he died just off the coast of Sierra Leone. On the same
day King Prempeh surrendered. (He was deposed and
deported.)

Meanwhile Princess Beatrice, at Osborne, had received
a telegram from Sir Francis Scott saying that the Prince had a
slight fever and had been sent back to the coast. Subsequent
telegrams were reassuring and told that he was on his way
to Madeira. On January 22 she received a telegram which
she expected to bring news that he had arrived at Madeira
where she hoped to join him for his convalescence. Instead
it announced his death.

The Queen wrote in her journal on that day: "A terrible
blow has fallen on us all, especially on my poor darling
Beatrice. Our dearly beloved Liko has been taken from us! . . .
What will become of my poor child? All she said in a trem-
bling voice, apparently quite stunned, was, 'The life is gone
out of me.' . . . There is such grief in the house. Dear Liko
was so much beloved. Went over to Beatrice's room and
sat a little while with her in her misery. What have we not all
lost in beloved, noble Liko, who has died in the wish to
serve his country! He was our help, the bright sunshine of
our home. My heart aches for my darling child. . . . God in
his mercy help us!"

Prince Henry's body was brought to Portsmouth in H.M.S.
Blenheim on February 3 and buried at Whippingham two
days later.

It was to this house of tragedy that Lady Lytton came less than a week after the funeral.

Osborne, Tuesday, 11 *February* 1896

All seems so different from the last waiting on account of the very great sorrow and the death of that good-looking charming Prince Henry of Battenberg at the war.

I had a very comfortable sunny journey for it was a lovely day, and the boat from Southampton was quite enjoyable. I met Gilbert the sculptor on the Pier, as he had been summoned by telegraph about decorations in the Chapel to Prince Henry, and had been staying last night at Osborne. We only had a few words.

[The Queen commissioned Alfred Gilbert, the creator of Eros, to design a Memorial to Prince Henry in Whippingham Church. Gilbert had already designed a memorial to the Duke of Clarence at St George's, Windsor, and while he was engaged on that work Prince Henry used often to visit him at his studio and they became great friends. It is related in Gilbert's biography by Isabel McAllister that Gilbert arrived at Osborne on a Saturday (evidently Saturday, February 8) and was commanded by the Queen to dine at Osborne on the Monday evening. He had brought an evening suit with him but not the required Court dress. Fortunately he had with him his moulder who had come to Osborne for a change of air and had been a tailor in his youth, and he undertook to convert Gilbert's evening trousers into knee-breeches by Monday. A lady's silk stockings were procured (Gilbert was a very small man), and shoes and buckles were eventually found after knocking up a succession of local shoemakers on the Sunday. In the meantime the Queen had been informed of his dilemma and had sent word that he need not wear Court dress, but now he was obliged to do so as he had no evening trousers. All turned out well, however. The Queen was let into the secret and remarked, "How clever!"

The Gilbert memorial tomb can be seen at any time in Whippingham Church which is always open. While doing the bronze work Gilbert put up a workshop beside the lych-gate and seven men worked there brazing the metal on a forge. The work was often carried on at night in cold weather, and at Christmas the Queen sent the workmen a hamper of delicacies.]

The carriage and footman met me, and the housekeeper [Miss Mitchie] came to the door on arriving at Osborne. I soon went to tea but always find it so strange to take the teapot and head of the table. Miss Phipps came first and it was nice seeing her, also Miss Drummond, Miss Moore and Mrs Grant,[1] and Fritz Ponsonby came in, but it was somehow rather solemn and stiff and everyone that you meet in deep black looks so gloomy. Miss Phipps told me a few details I wanted to know, and widow Princess Beatrice seems to be bearing up *wonderfully*. After tea I met Princess Christian in the passage and she said she would come to my room which she did and was most *touching* about her sister, and charming. She seems so tender to her poor sister and so loving.[2] The sadness of taking Princess Beatrice to his coffin on the *Blenheim* was intense, but she left her alone at first and when Princess Beatrice called her she seemed to have got quite calm, and she could repeat the responses then during the little touching service read at that time. The two Princesses sat by the coffin coming back on the *Alberta* and all was so quiet and reverent.[3]

The Prince's doctor [Dr Hilliard] and servant [Butcher, who had been with him for years] say they never thought he should recover when he was taken ill first, but on board ship

[1] Victoria Grant was an extra Woman-of-the-Bedchamber. She was a granddaughter of the Lord Elgin who had brought the Elgin Marbles to England, and a first cousin of the Viceroy. Fanny Drummond and Evelyn Moore were Maids-of-Honour.

[2] This was in contrast to the behaviour of another sister, Princess Louise, Marchioness of Lorne. Mr Pope Hennessy in his *Queen Mary* quotes a letter from the Duchess of Teck written from Osborne on February 9 saying: "Louise has alas ! *frisséd* her [Princess Beatrice] terribly by calmly announcing, that *she* (Louise) was Liko's *confidant* & Beatrice nothing to him, indicated by a *shrug* of the *shoulders* ! "

[3] Princess Beatrice went in the *Alberta*, the second largest of the Royal yachts, to receive the coffin from H.M.S. *Blenheim*, lying across the Solent. Besides Princess Christian, she was accompanied by the Prince of Wales, the Duke of Connaught and the Princes Louis and Francis Joseph of Battenberg.

he got better at first. Princess Christian talked so naturally and nicely for over half an hour, but I can't remember all the details. At eight I began dressing thinking the Queen would see me only just before dinner, and when my hair was all down, a knock came and the servant said, "The Queen wishes to see you." I put my hair up anyhow and dress on again, and was soon ready. The Queen was sitting by a comfortable writing table covered with photos, and began, "Dear Edith, I thought I should like to see you before dinner time," and I knelt by her and kissed her hand and tried to show her how much I felt for her. She began at once about the Prince. "And he stayed with you in Paris and he enjoyed it so much." The Queen said Princess Beatrice kept them all up and was so good, much better than she was able to be when the Prince Consort died. Then she said how terrible it was, but she had only for *one* day tried to prevent his going, and lamented because he had been such a joy in the house and helped to write for the Queen. But after a time she could talk of other things as well, the coming moves to Nice and Windsor and hoping to see Lord Salisbury soon; Mr Rhodes, the difficulties there had been etc.,[1] and sometimes even the beautiful smile broke across her face in the wonderful way it does.

We were only six ladies at dinner and it was very quiet and pleasant. Countess Feo Gleichen is so nice.[2] There came in two different dispatches summarising the Debates in the House of Lords and Commons, and even the sympathy for the death of the Prince was read out without emotion, but it was interesting. The evening was very dull as usual. The Queen went away to see Princess Beatrice part of the time,

[1] This was a few weeks after the Jameson Raid. Cecil Rhodes, Prime Minister of the Cape, had been implicated in the Raid and on January 5 had sent in his resignation.

[2] Feodore Gleichen (1861–1922) was the eldest daughter of Prince Victor of Hohenlohe-Langenburg, better known as Count Gleichen. She was the Queen's great-niece through her step-sister. Countess Feo was a well-known sculptress in her day and one of the few who worked in marble and stone. Among her works is the Queen Victoria Group for the Children's Hospital at Montreal; the Florence Nightingale Memorial at Derby; the Edward VII Memorial at Windsor; the Diana Fountain in Hyde Park; and the Kitchener Memorial at Khartoum which Gilbert described as the best memorial he had ever seen.

and Princess Christian was very sleepy. Mrs Grant is related to the Elgins and has been nine months in India so it amused me talking of that.

Wednesday, February 12

Dear Con's birthday and, Oh, such a lovely clear day and blue sky and sea like the Mediterranean. Princess Beatrice received me at half past two and was very calm and simple, but very miserable saying she had known nothing of the Prince being worse and then all was over, but she does not regret his having gone and is so wise and meek it is very touching. I told her how much help one gets but she cannot think of herself for many a long day. It calmed me to see her and yet, Oh, it is so sad.

I got a nice drive with Mrs Grant and Miss Moore. The Queen was very sad at dinner and hardly spoke, but we had some gentlemen.

February 13

Princess Beatrice left at six.[1] I went to Whippingham in the morning, and it is a peaceful Chapel where Prince Henry lies, and there were only a few wreaths on the stone which has been placed over the coffin and I was glad to see mine of South African Immortelles and leaves of the Silver tree, quite fresh. I also went alone to see where Sir Henry Ponsonby is laid. There is a lovely view from it.[2]

Went to see Countess Feo Gleichen's bust of Prince Henry [a statuette in his campaigning uniform]. It is very good even in the clay, and she is so clever. Prince Henry's servant was there, and told us many things, about the journey, the heat, and the illness. I drove with the Queen and Princess Christian who was *so* nice, and the talk was quite cheery, and the Queen seemed better, and I hope she may be less miserable now she is not with the Princess every day.

[1] She was going with her children to Cimiez, Nice, to the Villa Liserb lent by Mr William Cazalet. She was to be away a month, the longest she had ever been separated from her mother. She was crossing to Cherbourg on the *Alberta*.

[2] Sir Henry had died on January 21 at Osborne Cottage which had been his home for many years. The church of St Mildred at Whippingham had been designed by the Prince Consort and built in 1860.

At dinner I sat by *Sir* George Dennehy who was knighted K.C.I.E. to-day but only, I fancy, because of his choosing the Indian servants and helping with them, which seems hardly enough reason.[1]

February 14

Nice walk by the sea in the morning. Drive in the afternoon and called on Lady Cowell who has a striking beard on her chin.[2] Princess Christian came and had a chat after tea and was very amusing in my bedroom. Evening awfully solemn. Sir Henry Ewart [Crown Equerry] dined.

February 15

Called on Lady Edwards and Lady Bigge [wives of Sir Fleetwood Edwards and Sir Arthur Bigge] but found neither of them but met them after. Drove to West Cowes in the afternoon. Sat by the Queen at dinner but she does not seem to wish to talk much. Lord James [of Hereford] arrived and made the evening more cheerful.

[Lord James has left his own account of that evening at Osborne. He wrote in his diary on February 15: "At dinner Princess Christian sat on the Queen's right hand and I was placed next to her. We talked, as usual, in a very subdued tone, but the Queen often leant her head towards us and listened to our conversation. Just before leaving the dinner-room I told Princess Christian a little anecdote I had heard from Sir Henry D. Wolff. He is now our ambassador at Madrid, and when home on leave a few weeks ago he told me a supposed demonstration of the great intelligence of Spanish dogs. Lady Wolff possesses a favourite dog which dined every day with Sir Henry and Lady Wolff. One day, some friends dining, the dog's dinner was forgotten. It was too well behaved to scratch, so it trotted into the

---

[1] Maj.-Gen. Sir *Thomas* Dennehy had been Political Agent at Dholepore from 1879 to 1885, and was responsible for bringing the Munshi and other Indian attendants to England. He was now a Groom-in-Waiting.

[2] Lady Cowell, *née* Georgina Pulleine, was the widow of Sir John Clayton Cowell who had been Master of the Household until his death in 1894. She was an extra Woman-of-the-Bedchamber.

garden, selected and bit off a flower, and, returning, placed it on Lady Wolff's lap. Looking at it she found it was a 'Forget-me-not'. On my telling the Princess this remarkable tale, she at once said 'Oh, how pretty! Do tell that to Mamma.' The Queen looked responsively round, so I repeated the anecdote to her. She laughed heartily and said, 'But can it be true?' 'Your Minister at Madrid, Ma'am, is always remarkably accurate in his statements of facts,' I replied. 'Ah, so I understand,' said the Queen, with a very sly look."]

Sunday, February 16

Lord James talked very amusingly at breakfast, and said Chamberlain was most business-like in work, and he believed he would get the reforms done by Kruger for the Uitlanders. He only took ten minutes to decide to telegraph to stop Jameson.[1] There was a very quiet Service of Hymns and Communion in the Chapel and I felt so much for the Queen. She was so reverent and I was by her at the Altar. In the afternoon I drove with the Queen and Princess Christian and it was very nice and the Queen only a little sleepy at the end of the drive. She resented the grey sky and spoke of it three times. We had dinner only for the ladies and it was very quiet and the evening very dull but soon over.

February 17

The Queen's beautiful letter to the people appeared and is most perfectly expressed from her heart.[2]

Nice walk to the sea. Sir Arthur and Lady Havelock, a very scrubby couple going to Madras [as Governor], came to luncheon. Drove after, bitter cold wind but clear sky.

Admiral Fullerton was to have dined but never appeared.[3] The evening went off better.

---

[1] Dr Jameson had carried out his famous raid into the Transvaal on 30 December 1895. Chamberlain had immediately repudiated him and tried to turn him back but no one was able to stop him.

[2] This letter published in *The Times* is given in Appendix C on p. 157.

[3] Rear-Admiral Fullerton was in command of the *Victoria and Albert*, the largest of the Royal yachts, and of the *Alberta* which had taken Princess Beatrice to Cherbourg. He was knighted in 1899.

February 18

Heard at breakfast that the Admiral had been detained four hours in Osborne Bay with some of the machinery broken, and was cold and sick but landed at Cowes about eleven and stayed on board the *Alberta*. Horrid cold grey day but I took two walks to the sea alone which I enjoyed. I got a nice letter from Lady Salisbury who said of the Queen's letter in Monday's papers, "How charming the Queen's letter is. She has such a perfect genius for saying exactly the right thing in the best way. The power comes I am sure from her wonderfully sympathetic nature." Admiral Fullerton and Mr Smith[1] the clergyman from Whippingham came to dinner and the Queen seemed to like talking in the evening with the three gentlemen.

February 19

Lovely clear day and quite warm. Ash Wednesday: so Princess Christian found out for the ladies if they would be wanted and Harriet Phipps sent word that we were free to go to Church.

The Service was quite simple with the Commination but I prayed for Princess Beatrice with the Chapel before me containing all that made her life really happy. I walked back with Mrs Grant. In the afternoon I walked again a little alone. Dr Woods [Deputy Inspector-General of Hospitals and Fleets] of the *Alberta* dined, who had been with Princess Beatrice to Cannes. He said she slept well and could break down alone and then seem quite well before others, so the journey went off quietly. He is a very cheery pleasant man. The Queen was very quiet and sad all the evening having seen Dr Woods before dinner.

February 20

A wet day but the rain not very heavy. I watched the putting of luggage in the covered vans which are only moved on to the train, and the departure of many servants in different flies.

[1] The Rev. Clement Smith, M.A., M.V.O., born 1845; Rector of St Mildred, Whippingham 1895–1921; Canon of Windsor; Chaplain to Queen Victoria, Edward VII and George V.

We all left at 2.10 after luncheon, Colonel Byng [Equerry] being very fussy. Harriet Phipps and Mrs Grant came with me and the two Connaught Princesses (such charming young ladies of about twelve and eight with bright smiling faces and good manners, Princess Margaret and Princess Victoria Patricia, called Daisy and Patsy, they have a very smiling nice German Governess, Fräulein Kecker). The *Alberta* is such a lovely steam yacht and all was covered to get to her, but the rain ceased for the passage and the air was so soft.

When the Queen came on board the officers stood together, but all was silent and the Queen walked with Mustafa (who was arrayed in a most absurd grey coat like a dressing-gown, and quite unsuited to be near the Queen) and her head bowed with great sorrow and one thought of her last visit to the *Alberta* to receive Prince Henry's coffin.[1] Dr Woods talked to us. As we passed Ryde Pier I thought much of the dear mother and our last visit when T and I went over all her things in her empty room.[2] I stood up to see as much as I could but it was very misty. The landing at Gosport was also most quiet and silent. All had got into the train first except the Queen, Princess Christian, the young Princesses and the ladies. We had a nice saloon and the train went so smoothly one could read very happily.

We only stopped at Basingstoke to get on the Great Western, and all was quiet there also. We drove up to Windsor Castle as we left Osborne, and in shut carriages. There was a silent crowd on the way up, but all so sad. The ladies' sitting-room has been done up fresh, but in bad upholsteries, taste quite unsuited to the Castle, a pink striped paper very glaring, yellow–white dado; stuff for curtains a greenish ground with bunches of ugly roses, and a brown castellated screen with stamped brown velveteen. Miss Harbord [Maid-of-Honour] came to tea.

The dinner was so nice with only Princess Christian, Lady Biddulph, Harriet and I, and the talk was easy and

[1] She had gone down to Trinity Pier, Cowes, to meet the *Alberta* on February 4.

[2] Lady Lytton's mother had spent the last years of her life at Ryde and had died in 1890. T was Lady Lytton's eldest sister, Theresa, Mrs Charles Earle, author of *Pot Pourri from a Surrey Garden*, published in 1897.

general. In the evening the Queen only talked to Lady Biddulph of her great sorrow and pointed to where she had said good-bye to the Prince, which made the Princess and Harriet Phipps in a great state as the Queen has been always morbid about such things and they feel it will come back, but to me it was very natural. (Lord Salisbury says the anniversaries being so strictly kept is often a great inconvenience for fixing days of ceremony and the Queen would not have her Jubilee kept on the right day, the 20th of May, because "My uncle William IV had died that day.")

The Queen left her room very early and seemed so sad, and Princess Christian said at her tea, after arriving, she quite broke down.

February 21

I rushed down to Eton feeling much as if I was in a prison and longing to know how Nevsy [her son Neville] was, but the stupid servant told me wrongly that he was out. I left a note saying the Queen had asked if he had come up on Thursday evening [the evening of their arrival], so up he came at 6.30 and had a little tea and it was such joy seeing him.

The breakfast and lunch at Windsor are for the ladies and lord-in-waiting only. It was delightful having Lord and Lady Salisbury for dinner and I found them punctual in the corridor at nine, which one sometimes neglects as the Queen never comes till 9.20. Princess Victoria [Helena Victoria] and the Duke and Duchess of Connaught were there. I sat between Lord and Lady Salisbury. I saw the Queen looking well at Lord Salisbury, so I suppose she distinguishes well at the dinner table. The evening was very pleasant. Lady Salisbury went up to the Queen as soon as she had done her coffee. The Duchess of Connaught is very easy and talked to us all. The Queen made Lord Salisbury sit down by her later, which is very seldom offered.

February 22

We waited at breakfast with the Salisburys which is awkward when one has done eating, but the prayers being at nine, one begins breakfast at about 9.20. Lady Salisbury and I went on talking some time and went out together at twelve walking and saw the nice dogs in their well kept kennels.[1] There was a large luncheon before the Council and three Bishops' homage. The Duke of Devonshire [Lord President of the Council], Lord Arthur Hill [Comptroller of the Household], Sir M. White Ridley, the Bishops of Winchester [Randall Davidson], Newcastle [Edgar Jacob] and Hereford [John Percival]. I had to find out where to sit as best I could at the head of the table and felt very shy, but the Salisburys talked generally with the Duke of Devonshire so all went off well. Harriet Phipps kindly took a letter from Lady Londonderry to the Queen and got her consent at once to be Patroness of the sale of Irish Industries at Londonderry House.

I went down to Eton and had such a nice talk with Nevsy, who gave me an excellent tea, and I saw Donaldson[2] who as usual raved of both dear sons and said he had never had better boys. The dinner was dull, Princess Christian and her daughter, Thora [Helena Victoria], and Lord Salisbury was between them, also the Duke and Duchess of York. The Duke of York [later King George V] spoke loud and abused the German Emperor, not caring what he said, but the Queen was silent. In the evening the Queen only spoke to Lady Salisbury and retired early.

Sunday, February 23

We went to the Service in the Castle Chapel and the Bishop of Winchester (Davidson) preached telling us how to take sorrow in the right way but not mentioning Prince Henry's death too exactly, and the Queen told me in the evening, it was a great disappointment. The Salisburys left after luncheon. Dear Nevsy came up at three and we chatted and then took a little turn before St George's Chapel. It was bitterly cold though a lovely day. The boys' singing was lovely. Nevsy came back to tea and I had invited Miss Drummond and Lady Mary Lygon [Lady-in-Waiting to the Duchess of York] and Lord Edward Clinton [Master of the

---

[1] The kennels in the Home Park had been designed by Prince Albert in 1854.
[2] The Rev. S. A. Donaldson, Neville's housemaster at Eton.

Household] and Marcia Dalrymple, who arrived very out of health and looking so doubled up, but pretty. She said she was under a good doctor in London who did not want her to have any sister or friend with her while North is away at the Cape.[1] The dinner and evening were very dull as the Duchess of York stood all the evening and never spoke to any ladies. The Queen only talked to the gentlemen, the Bishop and Sir Fleetwood Edwards and General Gardiner [Groom-in-Waiting].

February 24

I went to see many things in the Castle which took two hours and a half. The Plate rooms so well arranged, the kitchens and offices (and so little originality comes out of them) very clean, quiet and well kept. The large fire roasts several legs of mutton at once and six chickens but they are very well done and also the plain puddings, but the vegetables are dull and also the entrées, fish and soup. Then we went to the Library and saw some of the very interesting Miniatures. One very authentic of Mary Queen of Scots, young and plain except for lovely pencilled eyebrows and good eyes. Sir Philip Sidney and Walter Raleigh very interesting.

The wind was awfully cold driving but we went to write our names in Cumberland Lodge [home of Prince and Princess Christian] and then saw the greenhouse at Frogmore. The evening was better as the Duchess of York came to speak and I suggested sitting. The Queen kissed me on leaving as I said I was going in the morning if her Majesty had no orders.

(The 11th March went to see the Yorks' baby Prince, a healthy, fine boy.)[2]

[1] Marcia Dalrymple was Lady Lytton's first cousin. She was a daughter of Sir Adolphus Liddell and married Colonel the Hon. North de Coigny Dalrymple who was severely wounded in the Boer War. She had just lost her baby daughter. The Dalrymples lived near Windsor.

[2] A later note in Lady Lytton's writing. Prince Albert (George VI) had been born on December 14, the day on which the Prince Consort and Princess Alice died. The Queen wrote in her journal on that day: "George's first feeling was regret that this dear child should be born on such a sad day. I have a feeling it may be a blessing for the dear little boy, and may be looked upon as a gift from God!"

Lady Lytton was again in waiting at Windsor in July of this year but she kept her diary for only seven days and the last page is so torn as to be partly illegible. The telephone was installed in Windsor Castle that summer, and there were lines not only from one part of the Castle to another but to the Post Office, Railway Station, Marlborough House and Buckingham Palace. Lady Lytton does not mention this innovation.

On July 3, the day she arrived, she noted that everyone was out except Lord Edward Clinton with whom she had "a nice talk about his excellent organisation and sad cases of drink amongst the servants as it always distresses one to see so much of it." And the next day she wrote: "There was a pleasant ladies' dinner. Princess Beatrice came and she is so good about talking to us. The Queen said in the evening, 'Edith, here is a bracelet for you,' and it was the one with the charming miniature of the Queen and inscription at the back, which I hope may always be kept in the family.[1] I was most grateful and kissed her Majesty's hand, and thanked her many times."

And on the 6th: "The Philip Curries [he was Ambassador at Constantinople] and the Wolseleys [he was Commander-in-Chief] came to dinner and were so interesting to talk with. The Queen thought Lady Currie would be very talkative but she was paralysed and silent.[2] I went to see the Wolseleys in their room Saturday morning and he talked of the bad news of Cavagnari's murder coming as they were marching to Pretoria and his saying to Colley. 'Well, what do you think?' 'That I ought to go at once, sir.' 'Well,' said Wolseley, 'that is just what I feel,' and he did come very quickly. Lord Wolseley looks so young [he was sixty-three] and sharp and cheery but he is so unpopular."

[Colonel Sir George Colley had been Lord Lytton's

[1] This bracelet and Lady Lytton's Orders are on show to the public at Knebworth House, Hertfordshire. The miniature of the Queen is in coloured enamels surrounded by small diamonds and opals, and the inscription reads : To the Countess of Lytton from her affectionate V. R. 1. 1896.

[2] Lady Currie was the poet and novelist, Violet Fane. She had a reputation for being an original and witty talker.

Military and then Private Secretary while he was Viceroy. At the end of the Zulu War, in July, 1879, Sir Garnet Wolseley, who was in command of the British troops in South Africa, requested that Colley should join him out there as his Chief of Staff. Lord Lytton let him go very reluctantly, for not only was he the perfect secretary but a great personal friend. On September 3 of that same year Sir Louis Cavagnari, head of the British Embassy to the Amir of Afghanistan, was massacred with all his staff at the Residency at Kabul. This was a terrible blow to Lytton who had been responsible for sending the Embassy. Colley was back in India early in November.]

Chapter Three

IN the autumn of 1896 Lady Lytton was again at Balmoral, but for the first fortnight of her waiting she was in attendance on the twenty-three-year-old Tsarina of Russia who came to England in September with the Tsar and their baby daughter, Olga, on a private visit to the Queen, after paying State visits to other Courts of Europe following their Coronation in May. The Tsarina had been Princess Alix of Hesse, the youngest surviving child of Princess Alice, Queen Victoria's second daughter who had died in a diphtheria epidemic in 1878. Princess Alix had become engaged to Nicholas, the Tsarevitch as he then was, on 20 April 1894, at Coburg where he had come for the wedding of Alix's brother, the Grand Duke Ernest of Hesse, to Victoria Melita, always called Ducky in the family, the daughter of the Duke of Coburg (formerly the Duke of Edinburgh).

Nicholas was four years older than Alix and had first been attracted to her when she was only twelve and had gone to Russia for the wedding of her sister Ella to Nicholas's uncle, the Grand Duke Serge (another instance of the Royal family marrying out of their generation), and he had first proposed to her five years before they became engaged. His parents were in favour of him marrying Hélène of Orléans, daughter of the Comte de Paris, which would have been very popular in Russia, but they cannot actively have opposed his marriage to Alix—although they must have known that there was hæmophilia in her family—because in December 1891 Nicholas was writing in his diary: "My dream is to marry Alix of Hesse. I have loved her a long time, but more deeply and fervently since the year 1889, when she spent six weeks in Petersburg. I have struggled for a long time against my feelings, and tried to persuade myself that it was an impossible thing, but since Eddy [the Duke of Clarence] gave up the idea of marrying her, or was refused by her,[1] it seems to me that the only obstacle between us is the religious question. There is no other because I am convinced that she shares my feelings."

Alix had been brought up as a strict Lutheran, and her conscience would not allow her to accept Nicholas, much as she loved him. In this refusal she had the support of her father, the Grand Duke Louis of Hesse, whom she adored; but even after her father's death in 1892, when she was left an orphan living at Darmstadt alone with her brother (her three sisters were all married) she could not reconcile her love with her religious principles.

Nicholas's grandfather, Alexander II, had been liberal in religion as well as in politics, and had not insisted on conversion to the Russian Church as a condition of marriage into the Romanoff family, but his son, Alexander III, the reigning Tsar, was extremely orthodox and there was no alternative for Alix but to change her religion if she married Nicholas.

Their problem still seemed insoluble on the day of Duke Ernest's wedding, April 19, and on that day the Empress Frederick, who was staying at Coburg, wrote to her daughter Sophie, the Duchess of Sparta: "Nicky was there looking very handsome. I wish I could tell you that everything is settled about him and Alicky, they both wish it but the religious question still seems the obstacle."

But the very next day the engagement was announced, and the Empress wrote again to Sophie: "Alicky was quite radiant, and beaming with joy. The moment Nicky arrived I saw by her face that she *would*—though it was so strange to refuse him at first, and to swear to everyone that though she was very fond of him she would never take him. Even my dear Mama [Queen Victoria was also at Coburg for the wedding] thought she would not accept him, she was so positive about it."

The Queen wrote about the engagement in her journal on April 20: "I was quite thunderstruck, as, though I knew Nicky much wanted it, I thought Alicky was not sure of her own mind. Saw them both. Nicky said, 'She is much too good

---

[1] She refused him in May 1890.

for me.' I told him he must make the religious difficulties as easy as he could for her, which he promised to do."

Kaiser William was among the host of royalty assembled at Coburg and is said to have persuaded his cousin Alix to accept Nicholas for the sake of Russo-German friendship. It is also maintained that Alix gave in because she did not like the idea of being supplanted at Darmstadt by a girl whom she had never liked and who was four years younger than she was. The Empress Frederick had described in a letter to Sophie, written in 1893, how she had gone over to Darmstadt and seen "Ernie and his sister quite alone in that big house, which was looking bright and cheerful, pretty and comfortable and well kept, just as it did when Uncle and Aunt were there surrounded by their children." There is something very cosy in this picture of a brother and sister on their own. The Empress Frederick also refers to Alix as having grown up without a mother (she was only four when her mother died) and being therefore a little spoilt "which has made her a little vain and conceited and affected at times."

One cannot see her playing second fiddle to her cousin Ducky; and there might also have been the understandable wish to catch the limelight during that imposing family gathering at Coburg. Or was it Nicholas's persistence that won her, or simply that she suddenly found him, with his newly grown beard, irresistible? She had not seen him before with a beard. (Nicholas's own account of the engagement is given in Appendix D on p. 159.)

But whatever the true reason, the fact that she did change her mind was a source of satisfaction to all her German and English relatives. The wedding was fixed for the following spring to give her time to prepare for her change of faith. She paid a long visit to the Queen in England in June and July, where Nicholas joined her for a month, and then settled down at Darmstadt and divided her time between learning Russian and receiving instruction from an Orthodox priest.

The Tsar fell dangerously ill in September and Nicholas was faced with a conflict between love and duty. He had planned to join Alix at Wolfsgarten, her brother's country house, but his mother wanted him to accompany her and his father to Livadia, the Tsar's villa on the Black Sea, where the doctors had advised him to go for his health. Duty regretfully prevailed, but early in October he was, to his great joy, allowed to invite Alix to Livadia. She was with him therefore when the Tsar died on October 31, aged only forty-nine. Some said that he died of Bright's disease; others thought that he was worn out with the fear of assassination. Prince Felix Youssoupoff maintained that six years before, when his train was derailed by nihilists, he had saved his family by propping up the shattered roof of the dining-car with his shoulders and had never recovered from the strain of this effort.

Two days after his death, on November 2, Alix was received into the Russian Church, and on the 26th she and Nicholas were married in St Petersburg. The wedding was hurried on because it was felt that the sooner an heir to the throne was born the better, and, according to the tradition of the Russian Church, no wedding could take place between Christmas and Easter; but coming so soon it seemed to be almost part of the funeral ceremonies and earned for Alix the soubriquet of the "Funeral Bride."

Thus at the age of twenty-six the tremendous burden of ruling autocratically an empire of eight and a half million square miles, the largest ever known, with a population of eighty-three million, fell upon Nicholas and his totally inexperienced wife of twenty-two. Alix never seems to have been popular in Russia, particularly with the aristocracy, and she only superficially got on with her mother-in-law, the Dowager Empress Marie Feodorovna, who had been Princess Dagmar of Denmark, a sister of the Princess of Wales, and who had disliked all Germans since the Schleswig-Holstein war of 1864. But instead of trying to win the people who did not welcome her, Alix shrank into herself and pretended not to care. She was very beautiful, but her beauty evidently lacked radiance, and she was also acutely shy, a shortcoming that is so often mistaken for haughtiness. Accounts vary as to how well she was able to speak Russian, but it is certain that she never became fluent in

French, a great disadvantage for it was the language of the Court.

Marie of Roumania, when Crown Princess, was among those who attended the Coronation in Moscow on 26 May 1896, and she writes of the Tsarina in her memoirs that "even at this supreme hour no joy seemed to uplift her, not even pride; aloof, enigmatic, she was all dignity but she shed about her no warmth." But Princess Marie, who was Ducky's elder sister, had little affection for her and seems to have taken no account of the fact that it was a five-hour ceremony and that she was standing almost the whole time weighed down by her coronation robes. Princess Marie Louise, on the other hand, who was her best friend, says that she "was a very wonderful person," but that "there was a curious atmosphere of fatality about her. I once said in the way that cousins can be very rude and outspoken to each other—'Alix, you always play at being sorrowful: one day the Almighty will send you some real crushing sorrows and then what are you going to do?'" And yet so bright was she as a little girl that she was nicknamed Sunny.

It did not add to her popularity when on 15 November 1895 she gave birth to a girl.[1] And then the following year, four days after the Coronation, came a terrible accident on the Khodynka Field just outside Moscow (now the Moscow Airport). During a huge Coronation fête the crowd broke through the inadequate police cordons, swarmed over the ground, which was cut up by unseen trenches, and thousands of people were suffocated or trampled to death. That evening there was to be a ball at the French Embassy which was part of the Coronation festivities and on which the French Ambassador, the Comte de Montebello, had been authorised by his Government to spend a million francs.

---

[1] In a letter to Lady Monkswell, Mrs Carnegie, whose husband was at the British Embassy in St Petersburg, wrote about the baby on 6 December 1895: "It was a disappointment to everyone except the Emperor & Empress that it was not the heir. They are so proud of themselves & each other & the baby that they think nothing could be more perfect. . . . The Empress had a very bad time, & I was told by one of her ladies that the Emperor was crying in the next room . . . they say the Empress is almost well & nursing her baby which has astonished all the Russians. It is so nice of her & I wish her subjects would appreciate her half as much as they should."

The Tsar and Tsarina made the mistake of not only failing to cancel the ball but of going to it themselves. There is a conflict of opinion as to why they did this. Their detractors say it was lack of feeling and imagination on their part; their supporters that Alix begged Nicholas to have the ball cancelled, or at least not to attend it himself, and indeed it was his own wish not to go, but that he was overruled by his advisers who considered that for their Majesties not to attend the ball might be construed as an insult to France. There seems to be a possibility that Nicholas was not aware until much later of the gravity of the accident. It happened before he appeared on the Khodynka Field to distribute food and gifts to the people, and every effort was made by the authorities to disguise it from him. It is even said that the bodies were shovelled under the grandstand on which he stood to get them out of sight. But whether it was their fault or not they were very much criticised for going to the ball, and the chief blame for such apparent callousness fell upon Alix. It got about that the "German Princess," the "Funeral Bride," was unfeeling as well as unlucky.

Whatever their political mistakes, though, whatever their lack of imagination in failing to realise the true state of Russia and continuing to rule as autocrats, Alix and Nicholas never failed in their love for each other. Her letters to him in 1915 and 1916, when he was away at the Front and she was middle-aged and the mother of five children, were passionately loving, and his to his "Beloved Sunny," as he usually called her, were no less so.[1]

This visit to Queen Victoria at Balmoral in September 1896 was Alix's first since her marriage. On her grand-daughter's wedding day the Queen had written in her journal: "How I thought of darling Alicky and how impossible it seemed that that gentle little simple Alicky should be the great Empress of Russia!" It must have been deeply gratifying to Alix to show her English aunts, uncles and cousins that from a poor relation (her parents had been left very badly off after the Prussian war against Austria in 1866

---

[1] Quotations from a few of these letters referring to their engagement are given in Appendix E on p. 161.

in which the duchy of Hesse-Darmstadt had sided with the Austrians), she had risen now to be the great Empress of Russia, with precedence before all the Royal ladies assembled at Balmoral apart from the Queen herself. Moreover, she was at the height of her beauty, having just done away with her unbecoming fringe, much to the satisfaction of her aunt, the Empress Frederick, who was always urging Sophie to do away with hers.

The Queen had not asked the young people to visit her entirely for the enjoyment of their company. Through personal contact with Nicholas she hoped among other things to counteract Russian hostility to the Anglo-Egyptian campaign for the reconquest of the Sudan. The Sudan had been abandoned in 1885 after the death of General Gordon, but now public opinion was strongly in favour of re-occupying the lost territory and avenging Gordon's murder. In March the defeat of the Italians by the Abyssinians at Adowa, had given England the excuse she needed for re-occupying Dongola, but the pretext of going to the help of the Italians was very thin and deceived nobody. If the Tsar could be won over it would be greatly to England's advantage. It was considered most important that Lord Salisbury too should have some private conversation with Nicholas, so although at first the Tsar's visit was to have been so private that no minister at all was to be there, it was decided on September 14 that Lord Salisbury's presence was essential. The Prime Minister intensely disliked going to Balmoral, for he suffered so much from the cold there, and therefore his secretary, Schomberg McDonnell,[1] took it upon himself to write to Sir Arthur Bigge: "I am sure you will forgive my mentioning it; but it is most necessary that Lord Salisbury's room should be very warm: a minimum temperature of 60 is the climate to which he is habituated, and a cold room is really dangerous to him. I am ashamed to bother you about so trifling a matter; but it is not so trifling as it seems."

In spite of the private nature of the visit the Prince of Wales saw the necessity of giving the Tsar a ceremonious welcome. (Nicholas was his nephew by marriage.) "I am

[1] Son of the 5th Earl of Antrim; afterwards Sir Schomberg McDonnell, K.C.B.

so anxious," he wrote to Sir Arthur Bigge, in a letter really intended for his mother (it was the practice of her sons to address her through the tactful intermediacy of her Private Secretary), "that the arrival should be marked with every possible compliment to the Emperor." He recommended that he should be met at Leith, the port of disembarkation for Edinburgh, with a guard of honour, and that a guard of honour should also be mounted at Ferryhill Junction (Aberdeen) and at Ballater Station. For a wedding present the Queen had made Nicholas Honorary Colonel of the Scots Greys, and therefore it was thought fitting that the 2nd Dragoons (Royal Scots Greys) should be the regiment in attendance.

It was also at the Prince of Wales's suggestion that the Russian Ambassador, Baron de Staal, was asked to stay at Balmoral for the visit. The Baron was a great friend of the Prince of Wales, and was very popular in England although he pretended that he could not speak English which he really spoke perfectly.

The Queen acquiesced in all the Prince's proposals. She was a little worried, though, about the Tsar's security, for there had been reports in the press about attempts against his life, and it was left to Sir Matthew Ridley to take every possible precaution for his safety. Sir Edward Bradford, the Commissioner of the Metropolitan Police, wrote to Bigge on the 22nd: "The Emperor is safer in England than anywhere else in the world, and of this you can assure the Queen and all concerned."

Lady Lytton and the Duchess of Buccleuch, the Mistress of the Robes, were the two ladies who went to Leith to meet the new Imperial yacht *Standart* which was making her maiden voyage. Enclosed in Lady Lytton's diary is an official programme stating that the members of the Queen's Household commanded to attend the Emperor and Empress were to assemble at Victoria Jetty at 10.30 a.m. on Tuesday, 22nd, to meet the yacht, and that their Imperial Majesties were to be received on their disembarkation by the Prince of Wales and the Duke of Connaught, and that the whole party was to set off at 2.30 from the landing stage to the railway station in five Royal carriages (the fourth carriage containing the baby, "her Imperial Highness the Grand Duchess Olga with two attendants"). There is also among Lady Lytton's papers a vellum-bound booklet, fastened with yellow silk, and emblazoned with the Tsar's arms, issued by the North British Railway, giving the times of the Imperial Train, a coloured map of the route, photographs of Edinburgh, the Forth and Tay Bridges (with descriptions), Aberdeen, Ballater and Balmoral.

We can imagine how welcome was the tea served at Ferrymill Junction at 5.31, especially as the train had rocked so much that the Empress was almost sick; and we know from the Queen's journal that the Imperial party arrived at the door of the Castle at the scheduled time of eight:

"The escort of Scots Greys came first, then the pipers and torch-bearers, and finally the carriage containing Nicky, Alicky, Bertie and Arthur. I was standing at the door. Nicky got out first whom I embraced, and then darling Alicky, all in white, looking so well, whom I likewise embraced most tenderly. She went round and shook hands with everyone standing in the hall. . . . We all went into the drawing-room. . . . The dear baby was then brought in, a most beautiful child and so big; after which Nicky and Alicky went to their rooms, and I quickly dressed for dinner."

It was a family dinner party for the Royalties that night. There was never before, and has never been since, such a family gathering at Balmoral. Every house in the neighbourhood was filled to capacity with royalty and their suites. There was no room at the Castle for Lady Lytton, so she stayed at Abergeldie five miles away.

The first page of her diary for this time is missing, but I have found a letter from her, addressed to no one in particular (though obviously meant for family circulation) and with no ending, describing the arrival of the Emperor and Empress at Leith.

Abergeldie Castle   *September 23, 1896*
I must give you a short account of my personal experiences yesterday though you will see in the papers what took place before the public. I was ready in good time [she was staying

in a hotel in Edinburgh] expecting some *change* even at the last, and by 10.20 the Duchess of Buccleuch came upstairs breathless and excited, and I heard after that at the last moment she had got a telegram to say the Prince of Wales would be at Leith by a quarter to eleven—(the Duchess had wired to me the night before that she would call for me). The Duchess was very nice driving to Leith and spoke of my sons—then of her own great sorrow, and told me how touched she was that Lord Grey had remembered to send a wreath for the anniversary of Lord Dalkieth's death as he was with him when the accident occurred.[1] The Duchess took a lovely bouquet to present to the Empress which was lucky as the one ordered by Lord Rosebery [Lord Lieutenant of the County] from Mentmore [Lord Rosebery's house at Leighton Buzzard] never arrived.

When we got to Leith the rain stopped a little and the water was smooth, but, Oh, the trying weather spoilt the effect of everything all day. The Prince of Wales, Duke of Connaught, Lord Rosebery and party arrived five minutes after we did at Leith landing place. The Prince of Wales looked so different in his Russian uniform but most comfortable with Astrakhan cap, knickers and boots, Norfolk jacket and splendid grey and red overcoat—not the least tight.[2] We went in a small steamer with no deck cabin but nice Turkey carpets and straw chairs, and had not to go down as holding up umbrellas was enough. The Emperor's yacht was a splendid looking large steamer. They had arrived at 8 a.m. It was now about half past eleven. As we approached we saw the Emperor (exactly like a skinny Duke of York— the image of him)[3] and a lovely slight lady in white serge

[1] The Duchess of Buccleuch's eldest son, Walter, had, on 17 September 1868, at the age of twenty-five, been killed in an accident while deer-stalking in the Achnacarry Forest, Inverness-shire. The Duchess had five other sons.

[2] The Prince of Wales was wearing the uniform of the Kieff (27th) Imperial Dragoons of which he had been made Honorary Colonel when he attended the Tsar's wedding in St Petersburg. The Tsar was wearing the uniform of the Scots Greys.

[3] The likeness between Nicholas II and his first cousin, the Duke of York, was so great that even their nearest relations were sometimes deceived. Nicholas was very short in contrast to the other male members of the Romanoff family who were exceptionally tall, almost giants.

with rather a mean little white bonnet, standing at the side of their ship, and they received us all most cordially.

The side of the Empress's face is unmistakably lovely but the full face is a little broad and German, but the charming expression makes up, so one is always in rapture with her—and a nice white feather boa was so becoming. They had had a smooth passage but both the Empress and Mlle Wassiltchikoff [Maid-of-Honour to the Empress] had not felt well enough to eat.

After some introductions and talk, we all sat down to luncheon—but first the gentlemen had their salt bits and liqueurs in Russian fashion at the sideboard, and I longed to taste all but was rather too *giddy* to run risks. The Emperor sat at the head of the table with the Empress on his left and the Duchess of Buccleuch on his right. The Prince of Wales next the Empress—then I with Lord Pembroke the other side. There was no whispering, and the Emperor and Empress being so young makes them so little alarming compared to old Royalties. The conversation was exactly what you might suppose, but the Duke of Connaught was the most cheerful. He mentioned with a hearty giggle that he always thought when a boy "Arthur's seat" had been given that name because he sat there as a child! One longed for "haute politique" to be discussed, and when one looked at the very young Czar it seemed more than ever ridiculous of the papers to say that all depended on him for decisions in the Eastern Question. Count Worontzoff [Minister of the Court] has a cross Russian face with a hideous white Astrakhan cap but he was very pleasant to talk with. There were several different Russian dishes and the more foreign style of luncheon so superior to our heavy English ones.

The Prince of Wales told me about the Hamburg time and his visits and Cara Batten's young man who hopes to have a place in the City which will give him £2000 a year—but the *hope* may not be realised![1] He asked after our dear sons and

[1] Cara Batten was the daughter of George Maxwell Batten, C.S.I. The Lyttons while they were in India had known the Battens well. Mrs Batten's elder sister was the Hon. Mrs Edward Bourke, a great friend of the Prince of Wales. They were daughters of Lieut.-General Cliffe Hatch, C.S.I. Cara Batten's "young man" was Austin Harris, who became a Director of Lloyds Bank and

was very nice all day to everyone. I marvelled as much as ever at their power of eating and mixing wines.

The Empress ate very little but is not expecting another child as was said. After luncheon the little Grand Duchess Olga, aged ten months appeared, and, Oh, you never saw such a darling as she is—a very broad face, very fat, in a lovely high Sir Joshua baby bonnet—but with bright intelligent eyes, a wee mouth and so happy—contented the whole day. She smiled at me very happily, and is quite an old person already—bursting with life and happiness and a perfect knowledge how to behave.

Mlle W. showed us the Emperor and Empress' cabins, and the whole ship, fitted out in Denmark, is in the best taste. The dining room was grey satin curtains and silver everywhere. The Emperor's Cossack servant was a splendid sight with a long beard and so huge. The priest of the ship was also very remarkable, and the odd cheer to the Emperor and Empress as they said "good bye" very odd—like "Hish, hash, hesh" said well together as we play it. It was raining as we left the ship but not heavily to hurt one in any way, and in the small steamer we went in the nice cabin below where was a characteristic bit of food on the table—a pie, a bottle of champagne and some fruit. Luckily no one had to taste of it. We all talked of the baby and weather but I felt so inclined to go off in hysterics when the Russian guns banged a salute to the Prince of Wales, I had to keep very quiet.[1]

The landing stage was quite unworthy of our great country but we don't do these things well, and Lord Rosebery jokingly said it was the fault of the Government—Lord Salisbury should have undertaken it—though he had the honesty to allow no Government could do what they liked, but the local authorities had no money. However the humble man who had done his best with only a week's notice was

was knighted in 1920. He married Cara on 26 October 1896, before the £2000 a year "place in the City" had materialised, for at the time of his marriage he was earning only £700 a year in his father's shipping firm of Harris & Dixon.

[1] She could not bear the sound of guns. In India, whenever a salute was given to her husband, the Viceroy, she suffered dreadfully.

quite pleased with himself as there was red, white and blue—
and black and yellow, and a really good reception place with
a lovely boudoir behind. The reception of the Mayor was
the next thing—and they had evidently not got over their
frightful jealousies which had caused scenes for many days,
as the Provost of Leith mumbled that he would leave it to a
much greater gentleman than himself to say the appropriate
words of welcome, but the wife of the Provost of Leith gave
a lovely basket of flowers.[1] The Provost of Edinburgh could
not keep up his dignity as he was a much shyer, more awkward
man, and I could not hear much he had to say but he presented
a splendid gold casket. The Emperor very shyly whispered
a few words of thanks, but he ought to learn to do this sort
of thing better. She smiles, but neither of them take trouble
enough to bow to all assembled as our Queen did *so* well.

Mlle W. and I were in a saloon to ourselves during the
railway journey and there is nothing of any interest to report.
The drive in procession for about fifteen minutes with heavy
rain was rather trying but the very seedy looking Russian
Ambassador, de Staal, said I saved his life by covering his
knees with my fur cloak. He had *no* umbrella and his seedy
uniform hat looked extra draggled.

It poured with rain all the time on the journey but was
so quiet and resting. Mlle had a sick headache but I did all I
could to help her. She had taken cocaine powders and the
effect had not been happy—and she wanted to sleep it off.

The Ballater station was quite lovely with electric light
and pretty decorations and the Guard of Honour there so
good. The troops at Leith all seemed the youngest, feeblest
boys. We had our carriage shut as it was cold and rainy from
Ballater, but the Imperial carriage was open at the beginning
and end. The fires on all the hills, and torchlight processions
fascinated me, but my companions in the carriage would
not be excited over it.

The Queen and all came to the Hall, but they were moving

[1] The Provost of Leith was John Bennet. By "the Mayor," Lady Lytton
meant the Lord Provost of Edinburgh, Provost in Scottish burghs being the
equivalent of Mayor in English burghs. The Lord Provost of Edinburgh was
Andrew M'Donald, born 1836. He was Lord Provost from 1894 until 1897
when he was knighted.

away when we got in, but all went to the drawing room to be received by turns. Her Majesty (the Queen) was rosy and looked *so* well as she always does up here. The Connaughts have always the best manners of all. It was nice seeing all the Household but they were rather too awe-struck and interested to be able to speak much. There were carriages to bring our party back here directly, to this Castle, which is ideally comfortable and I have a lovely big room. Slept well but feel tired, for yesterday was a long day but I was so interested and never sleepy.

Her diary now begins:

September 26
This little Abergeldie Castle is so comfortable and the breakfasts with the two charming Connaught Princesses, Prince Drino of Battenberg [Princess Beatrice's eldest son, Alexander, aged ten, afterwards Marquess of Carisbrooke] and the very nice governess [Fräulein Kecker] are the pleasantest part of the day, and I can spend a very quiet morning in this nice large sitting-room. My duties all day are only two meals at Balmoral and going out with Mlle W. [Catherine Wassiltchikoff]. I get back here to a quiet tea.

It is a great help to watch Lady Churchill but I feel I did all much the same from what she told me.[1] But I miss even the little duty of helping the Queen in the evening and only get a few words with her. I sit at the other end of the table at luncheon by Lord Edward Clinton who always amuses me with details of his administration. The under servants are so fearfully crowded at Balmoral in their rooms. Four laundry maids have to sleep in one bed in a tiny room, and he is hoping the iron houses which are now hired for £500 may be purchased at £50 [sic] and the maids made comfortable. I hear ninety horses were used on the 22nd, the day of arrival, and the turnout of each carriage was perfect. After dinner the 23rd, the Duke of Connaught told me of Sir N. O'Conor refusing to go to the thanksgiving service

---

[1] Jane, Lady Churchill, the widow of the second Lord Churchill who died in 1886, was a Lady-in-Waiting. She had been with the Queen for nearly fifty years and was perhaps her most intimate friend.

at the Protestant English Church at St Petersburg on the Queen's birthday, which he and the Duchess attended. I am afraid he cannot take in his duties by this. We never thought of refusing to attend any ceremonies in the Roman Catholic Churches where we were abroad.[1]

On the 24th we had a lovely day and I took Mlle W. to call on the Clanwilliams at Birkhall and found them as full of chatter and life as before, with several visitors. Then to Glenmuick where Alice Glenesk was alone with Algy's sister [Harriet Borthwick]. She is evidently bursting with pride and delight of Royal favours and visitors (the Duke and Duchess of York, Duke of Cambridge and Hohenlohes[2] are staying there) but she complains of the Duke of York having four menservants and the Duchess two maids, and fifty-eight people in the house to think of altogether. Ernest[3] is there also, and daily shooting but came here yesterday morning and is not looking well, but this air does one immense good. The Glenesks dined at the Castle in the evening and were treated with much favour by all, and Algy talked with Queen and Emperor with smiling familiarity. He told me the Queen was much delighted with his present to H.M. of a tortoise-shell paper knife with two gold coins on the handle, the Queen's head just covering George III's.[4] I dined with the household, it was so cheery and nice and went to the Royal circle after.

[1] Sir Nicholas O'Conor, who was a Roman Catholic, was Ambassador at St Petersburg from 1895 to 1898. The Duke and Duchess of Connaught had stayed with him for the Tsar's Coronation in May. It was stated in the *Daily Courier* of April 23 that the English Government had given him £6000 towards defraying his expenses attendant on the Coronation, out of which he had to rent a house in Moscow, which alone cost £1200 for three weeks, and pay all the expenses of the Duke and Duchess of Connaught while they were there, whereas the French Government had given their Ambassador, the Comte de Montebello, £40,000.

[2] Princess Victor of Hohenlohe-Langenburg, widow of the Queen's nephew through her step-sister, Feodora, and her youngest daughter, Helena.

[3] Colonel Villiers, Lady Lytton's only brother. He stayed every autumn with the Glenesks.

[4] The occasion of this gift was the attainment by the Queen on the 23rd of the longest reign in English history, and in spite of the fact that she did not want any demonstrations until the following June, when her official Diamond Jubilee was to be kept, telegrams of congratulation kept pouring in all day. The previous longest reign had been that of George III.

Yesterday, the 25th, I had a perfect walk in the evening up the hill opposite Abergeldie on the wild heather ground after passing dashing streams which always reminds me of Corndavon (I with Lord Ward) days, and the wind on the height nearly blew one down but it gives one as much strength to face life as the roots of the dear heaths always alone up there. There was a lovely complete rainbow at the head of the valley towards Ballater, and at eight there was a lunar rainbow, which I wish I had seen, it was like an opal in colour the Duke of Connaught told me. He killed four stags yesterday and the Duke of York five, but the Emperor though in the best place got none. The Empress talked to me a long time after dinner and was so nice. Like anyone else she has had nurse troubles and the first she had was rude and domineering, never even bowing to the Emperor. The one she now has is housekeeper in a Russian family and she cannot keep her, but she is nice.

Saturday, September 26

In the evening it was nice to see Lord Salisbury talking to the Empress, and Princess Beatrice soon made them sit down, then later the Emperor sat talking with him.

Sunday, 27th

The most awful stormy morning but all was arranged for going to Kirk so we all went and got no harm in shut carriages for her Majesty never gives in. It was very interesting seeing the two pews full of the Royalties and the Emperor and Empress standing by the Queen even in the Scotch Kirk, where all is simple and reverend, and the prayer for their Majesties was good, but the Sermon so dull, I could not say what it was. The Duke of Connaught is so easy and nice and came home with us, the three English ladies [Miss Phipps and Lady Churchill were the other English ladies]. Mlle W. did not come having a cold, but the Russian Gentlemen[1] came so the Greek Church is very liberal.

[1] Count Worontzoff-Daschkoff, Minister of the Court; Major-General Prince Dimitri Galitzin, A.D.C.; Major-General Count Paul Benckendorff, Marshall of the Court and Head of the Tsar's Household. He was a brother of the Count Benckendorff who later became Russian Ambassador in London.

I came home after lunch as Mademoiselle was going out with the Russian gentlemen, and I had a nice walk with Colonel Carington and Colonel Alexander[1] (*private*—such a funny childish type of simple tactless man) up the wood and hill opposite this, and, Oh, I love the hill air. The Prince of Wales talked to Lord Salisbury near me in the evening and I heard him say Lord S must find the Emperor very nice, and to the Duke of Connaught Lord S said, "He is very different from the other Emperor!" The Prince of Wales hoped Lord S would talk to Staal also (though he has gone to Birkhall). One can only pick up little things and draw one's own conclusions, but the Ambassador Staal was in tearing spirits Sunday night and Monday, and all the Royalties all most smiling and happy together.

Monday, September 28

Lovely cold day and we got a drive to Braemar and I always love that road it is so lovely. The Prince of Wales was very jolly in the evening and has been the greatest help all the time, and they had had a pleasant grouse drive and tea at Glenmuick to reward Glenesk for sending the luncheon to the Mountain. Ernest was presented by the Prince of Wales to the Emperor and he told me of this. Alice made a scene with poor ladies, who brought out birthday books, though I suppose *she* got the Emperor's signature. (I have got all that were interesting for Vic's book.) The Staals and Clanwilliams dined.

Tuesday, 29*th*

There was Photographing before lunch, a group of seventeen of attendants and Household, but only a Ballater man, so I fear not very likely to be good. Dear old Staal was so cheery.

I came back as Mlle W. went out with Mlle de Staal after ordering a separate lunch which seemed very unnecessary, but she has much courage in getting all she wants, and I had

[1] Lieut.-Colonel the Hon. Walter Alexander, Commanding the Scots Greys, was in attendance upon the Emperor; Lieut.-Colonel the Hon. William Carington was Equerry-in-Waiting.

HOUSEHOLD GROUP
BALMORAL, SEPTEMBER 1896

1. Presumably Mlle Wassiltchikoff.
2. Colonel Carington.
3. ?
4. Sir Arthur Bigge.

5. Sir James Reid.
6. ?
7. Colonel Davidson.
8. Presumably Hon. Ethel Cadogan.
9. Lady Lytton.
10. ?
11. Hon. Harriet Phipps.
12. ?
13. ?
14. ?
15. Viscount Churchill.
16. Lord Edward Clinton.
17. ?

The editor would be grateful to any reader who can identify the unnamed
members of the group.

Oh, such a lovely walk right up a mountain the other side of the river, all heather and wildness, only meeting four sheep and two grouse!

Sir James Reid (doctor) told me in the evening the cataracts on the Queen's eyes had been improved by some Belladonna ordered by Pagenstecher,[1] which dilated the pupils and dispersed the film, but it was only a temporary good, and gradually the film would cover the ball of the eye and the sight be clouded over, and though the Queen says now she will have no operation, she may change her opinion when the sight fails. [She never had an operation.] At present I rejoice that she can see much more. Sir James is so open I like him much, now many at Court are so "boutonné" as if they knew many secrets they will not tell.

September 30

Mlle W. went after lunch to Edinburgh with the Staals for two days. I drove with the ladies (after looking at *objets d'art* in the Prince Consort's room which always interests me), Churchill and Phipps, who were so nice and they had tea with me at Abergeldie. I had a pleasant dinner between Sir A. Bigge and Lord Edward Clinton who manages all the household wonderfully and amuses me with details. The Prince of Wales had told one of the pages how well all was done, but not to Lord Edward himself. The Queen influences the Emperor and Empress to be much on their majesterial dignity I think, which is a mistake but they will come out of it no doubt by degrees!

All had been to Mar Lodge, and the Emperor had neuralgia and a swollen face so did not come to dinner. The Empress spoke to me at the end as I went up to offer my services and said I might go to her in the morning about some letters.

[1] Professor Pagenstecher was a famous oculist of Wiesbaden ("one of the greatest oculists in Europe," according to the Queen). Princess Christian had taken a cure under him in 1889. He had seen the Queen at Osborne on 24 August. He saw her again on 7 May 1899, and on 6 May 1900, on both of which occasions he said that her eyes were no worse; and he was at Osborne a few days before she died. He stayed with Princess Christian at Cumberland Lodge when he came to England.

October 1

Glorious summer's day. I sat out in the garden from ten to eleven, and Lochnagar [the mountain to the South of Balmoral] was so lovely with heather red on the nearer hill and dark blue to the highest peak. I did long to fly to it. I went to Balmoral in a nice open trap, and saw the Empress in the library. She gave me the usual kind of letters sending books that come every day to people in high position from half-maniacs who have nothing better to do, one on nursing, one of Mrs Kingsley's birthday book and so on. Then the Empress spoke so nicely about her baby, nurse and education, fearing Princess Beatrice did not see enough of her children. Harriet Phipps came with me driving and we went on the Corndavon road up on the moor and it was lovely and peaceful. In the evening the Queen spoke very kindly about our popularity in Paris, that I ought to give Lady Monson[1] hints to help her, etc., and she told me she did not like the Prince of Wales racing (his horse [Persimmon] won at Newmarket today) and that it encouraged it so much in others, and the Prince Consort was so against it, and quite distressed when the Prince even put in to a lottery. But it makes the Prince happy and is perhaps a better excitement than others.[2]

The Empress looked lovely in pink, and she told me a pear-shaped diamond drop on her neck was "a little Easter egg from the Emperor."

The ladies and gentlemen all round mix up better now so the evenings are less stiff. The Empress told me I might see the little Grand Duchess in her bath at seven to-morrow evening.

October 2

Still nice warm day and the garden is so nice after our merry breakfasts with Prince Drino and the Connaught

[1] Wife of Sir Edmund Monson, who was Ambassador in Paris from 1896 to 1905 when he was created a Baronet. Lady Monson was a daughter of Major James Munro, Consul-General at Montevideo.

[2] Persimmon won the Jockey Club Stakes, defeating Lord Rosebery's Sir Visto by two lengths. (He had won the Derby on June 2.) The Prince had gone to Newmarket for the event, which had annoyed the Queen, but as the race was worth £10,000 his wish to be there, even in the middle of the Tsar's visit, is very understandable.

BALMORAL, SEPTEMBER 1896

Standing from left to right: Duke of Connaught, Princess Patricia of Connaught, Prince of Wales, Prince Charles of Denmark, Duchess of Connaught, Princess Victoria of Schleswig-Holstein, Princess Victoria of Wales, Tsar, Princess Margaret of Connaught. *Seated*: Princess of Wales, Tsarina, Duchess of Fife, Princess Charles of Denmark.

Princesses and German governess. Came back after lunch at the Castle hoping to rest but Alice Glenesk, Princess Hohenlohe and Mr da Costa drove up before I could get in and I had to entertain them till five with chat and tea. Lord Edward came here on business with the housekeeper, then I walked back to Balmoral with him, and Mlle W. joined us full of her expedition to Edinburgh and Aberdeen, and chatting most pleasantly. At half past six I got a trying message that I need not go to the baby's nursery, and heard after the Queen was there, but I was *so* disappointed. I could not get back to dress till half past seven and then had a rush to be in time. Lord Edward told me the Emperor had given £1000 for the servants which was very grand.

Saturday, October 3

Went to Balmoral at twelve to walk with Mlle W. and we went to the Prince Consort's Cairn which was a stiff climb but by a good path and we had Mademoiselle's new dog "Glen" who is such a dear and I felt sorry for him to be leaving the bonny Scotch mountains.[1] Mademoiselle talked of her love of the Italian Poet Dante and she quoted much very cleverly but had not learnt from an Italian. She talked of books of all nations and told me about her life in Russia and was very nice and intelligent. I told her the Empress said she had got to know her so much better on the journey and that she hoped she was not shy now, and this pleased Mademoiselle. After lunch there was nothing more to do so I went back to Abergeldie to read and dress, and the maid had to go at eight. Colonel Carington and Mr Tufnel [a Gentleman-at-Arms] drove back to Abergeldie for an 8.30 household dinner (the royalties dined alone). Lord Pembroke [the Lord Steward] proposed the health of the Queen, and Emperor (no Empress by mistake) and our

[1] The Cairn is a granite pyramid, thirty-five feet high, on Craig Lowrigan, completed ten years after the Prince's death and inscribed "Albert the Great and Good, raised by his broken-hearted widow." Lady Lytton seems to have missed an historic occasion by going for this walk, for the Queen wrote in her journal on October 3: "At twelve went down to below the terrace, near the ballroom, and we were all photographed by Downey by the new cinematograph process, which makes moving pictures by winding off a reel of films."

guests in different toasts with cordiality. I must mention that the Empress sent for me when I arrived in the library, and gave me a lovely diamond brooch with a pearl drop,[1] and said, "I thought it would look well on your black," and a photo of the Emperor, Empress and baby, and was most kind.

We departed about a quarter to ten, the Queen only received the Russians.[2] It was a warm evening but damp, so we had our carriage shut luckily to Ballater. The torches were round the entrance but did not accompany the Emperor's carriage I believe. The Grand Duchess Olga, the baby, in a pink flannel dressing gown looked quite lovely at her carriage window when we visited her, and the Emperor and Empress visited her after they arrived. Then very soon the special train moved slowly out to the sound of the Russian National air. The Duke and Duchess of Connaught were in the train. I did not get much sleep, only between four and seven. (I woke to realise my thirty-second wedding day.) Breakfast at a quarter to nine was very well done at Preston with lovely flowers and fruit on the table and a basket of white flowers sent by the Mayoress and ladies of Preston to the Empress. The baby called "Papa" after, on the platform, and was so good though only eleven months. Quiet day in the train though Mlle W. was rather talkative and wanted to read out loud but the noise was too great for me to take it in. We had two sleeping carriages and saloon in the middle. It poured with rain but people came to the fields and stations to wave a hearty welcome. Luncheon at Oxford was very well done, also, such good food, lovely orchids and fruits again. Lord Harris came and was well received though I heard after that he offended the Emperor as Czarevitch at Bombay.[3]

Lord Churchill [Lord-in-Waiting, Lady Churchill's only

[1] This brooch, which Lady Lytton is wearing at her throat in the picture opposite page 152, was stolen a few years ago from Pamela, Countess of Lytton who inherited it.

[2] Lady Lytton was accompanying the Tsar and Tsarina to Portsmouth. They were going to Paris on a State visit.

[3] In 1890, Nicholas had been sent on a two-year tour of the Far East. Lord Harris had been Governor of Bombay 1890–95, and was now a Lord-in-Waiting.

THE TSAR AND TSARINA WITH THE
GRAND-DUCHESS OLGA

son] kindly took Mademoiselle just to see the outside of Christ Church as she was longing to see everything she could, and he presented the Empress and Mademoiselle with lovely bouquets. Much rain at Portsmouth also but luckily just stopped for our getting out and going on board the *Polar Star* Russian yacht. The guns were awfully near and trying. As we were beginning tea, the Evening Hymn was played at sunset, and all stood up (I was so afraid of not getting my tea) and all the men do so, which is better than a Church Service. The Queen's yacht *Victoria and Albert* was most comfortable just next the Russian yacht but a stove had been lit in my cabin so it was too hot for me to rest though very tired.[1] Dinner at eight on board the Russian yacht and we went in a launch not to get our feet wet. It was splendidly done for about sixty people I should think. I sat between the Duke of Connaught and Admiral Bedford [Sir Frederick Bedford, 2nd Sea Lord]. The Emperor drank the Queen's health, and the Duke of Connaught asked permission to drink the Emperor's though his guest, and the Emperor appealed to the Empress who seemed very pleased. We listened to the excellent band with cloaks on after dinner upstairs, but it was *very* chilly, then the Governor's daughter's book was brought for signatures as usual and as they were signing in the small deck-room I saw the Empress give the Emperor such a loving look, I am sure she is devoted to him. I wonder how long they will be spared to each other, and happy. He looks delicate, but has never been ill.[2]

About ten the Emperor and Empress made everyone file past them and leave and then they came on to our yacht and went all over it, and when the Empress got to the passage to the smoking room below she said, "And here we always ran as children," so she ran again joyously. I slept fairly till four and was up at six to see from the deck the departure of the Russian yacht. The officers and men stood in rows but no hearty cheer was raised, but the guns made an

[1] In Frederick Ponsonby's words, the *Victoria and Albert* was "a paddle-wheel steamer, picked out in black and gold, with deck cabins of gleaming white and funnels of light buff."

[2] The Tsar's account of this visit to England, written to his mother, is given in Appendix F on p. 164.

awful noise. One feared the passage to Cherbourg would be very bad as a gale had been blowing for two nights and the Duke of Connaught could not go to Spithead in his launch. One felt relieved the visit was so successfully over and some of us would have exclaimed "thank goodness" but Prince Galitzin was left behind to return to Russia and came to breakfast at nine with the Duke and Duchess of Connaught, the Duchess of Albany[1] and suites. I went to London with Colonel Carington and Prince Galitzin and got there by twelve. The English Fleet accompanied the two Russian yachts half way, then the French Fleet took charge after both Fleets had saluted each other (who-shall-we-choose-to-fetch-him-away-position,[2] as Con said). Dear Liz [Lady Lytton's twin sister, Lady Loch] met me and took me to 41 Portland Place, where I rested, and Con and Vic came to cheer me till six and we had nice talks, then I lay down, had a bath and supper meal and went off to the 11 p.m. night express to Aberdeen and slept well though a very cold night and the swaying very alarming at the end of the train. Nice walk at Aberdeen about eleven, and found some lines of Wordsworth's so suited to the Empress in the waiting-room.

> "A perfect woman, nobly planned
> To warm, to comfort and command,
> And yet a spirit still and bright
> With something of an angel light."

October 6

My return to Balmoral was rather awkward but all very kind. Lady Churchill was still in her room. I met Princesses Beatrice and Victoria [Helena Victoria] in the passage and they were sympathetic, then Ethel Cadogan [Maid-of-Honour] took me in, but Harriet Phipps soon came and gave me her bedroom, and I rather longed to be alone after the long journey and it was a great rest till an early tea, and Lady Churchill started with Princess Victoria at five. The Queen was very kind in the evening and said the Emperor of Russia told her he was much too busy to be able to enjoy

---

[1] The widow of Queen Victoria's fourth son, Leopold, who had suffered from haemophilia and died in 1884.
[2] As in the game of "Nuts in May."

his private life with his wife. He would not decide yet about replacing Lobanoff.[1] Harriet Phipps announced that she had heard from Lady Biddulph of the birth of the young Ampthill's son.[2] Lord George Hamilton [Secretary of State for India] was very nice and talked to me about India. He fears the scarcity will be very wide-spread, from the failure of crops.

October 7

Pleasant breakfast. Lord George Hamilton makes even others talk out more, and Sir Arthur Bigge spoke of the letters about the Russians in Paris (their time at Balmoral he speaks of as "during the Russian occupation") and of Lord Harris offending the Emperor as Czarevitch on a matter of precedence in India. A lovely day and morning walk with Ethel Cadogan and Mizer Jap wee dog. I drove with the Queen and it was very cold. Pleasant dinner and evening.

October 10

I have had two more drives but in shut carriages as it has been so wet. Yesterday the Princess of Wales, Princess Victoria and the Prince and Princess Charles of Denmark arrived as we came in at half past five and they are so civil in the evening.

[The Prince of Wales's youngest daughter, Maud, had married on July 22 her first cousin, Prince Charles of Denmark. In 1905 he was elected King Haakon VII of Norway. Prince and Princess Charles had been staying at Mar Lodge for the Russian visit. Princess Victoria was the second daughter; she never married. She was twenty-three.

[1] Prince Lobanoff, who had been the Russian Foreign Minister and a great anglophobe, had died suddenly on August 30 while on a visit with the Tsar and Tsarina to the Emperor Franz-Joseph of Austria. It was hoped by the Prince of Wales that he would be succeeded by Baron de Staal, and he asked the Queen to suggest this to the Tsar, but she thought it wiser not to interfere. Lobanoff was eventually succeeded by Count Mouravieff who was also an anglophobe and what the Empress Frederick described as a "sly fox."

[2] Oliver Ampthill, 2nd Baron, had married Lady Margaret Lygon in 1894. Their son, John Russell, was born on October 4 and was later to be involved in the famous Russell divorce case.

The Empress Frederick admired the Princesses Victoria and Maud of Wales far more than two other nieces of hers, the Tsarina and her sister, the Grand Duchess Serge, who were said to be two of the most beautiful women in Europe. Victoria and Maud "are more graceful and more natural," she wrote to her daughter Sophie in 1894, "and so much more agreeable and bright. I think they are more clever too. How I wish they would marry. It does seem a shame for such charming girls not to have homes of their own. They would make such perfect wives and mothers." It was not through lack of opportunity that Princess Victoria never married. Her parents had hoped that she would marry her first cousin, Prince Christian of Denmark, Prince Charles's brother and the eldest son of the Crown Prince Frederick, but Victoria "would not hear of it."

Lady Paget, Ambassadress at Rome and Vienna, was also a great admirer of this least known of Edward VII's daughters. She wrote of her while staying at Sandringham: "Princess Victoria was charming, her *espiègle* expression and large long eyes making her infinitely attractive. I am told that her unselfishness and generosity are quite marvellous. She is a good musician and splendid rider." She was utterly devoted to her mother which is perhaps one of the reasons why she never married.]

There was a ceremony after lunch for the Lord Provost from Edinburgh [Andrew M'Donald] and many other gentlemen to present a casket with their congratulations on Princess Maud's marriage. It was lucky she was there, but it was awkwardly managed and after bumping on their knees the Queen was told not to give her hand to be kissed, and after the Queen said, "I know they expected to kiss my hand, but I was particularly told not to do so." The Queen said, "I thank you and I am so glad my dear grandchildren are here with me."

Sunday, October 11

It snowed heavily and was quite deep all round the castle as well as on the hills. Service in the Chapel, dull sermon.

I went for a walk after in the morning but got wet, so did not go later. Pleasant dinner but heard that the Archbishop of Canterbury (Benson) had died suddenly in Church. Lord George Hamilton was very pleasant at dinner.

October 12

Heard the Archbishop of Canterbury had passed away in Church while the absolution was being said, in the most beautiful way that could be, for so holy a man.[1]

I drove in the morning with Miss Knollys [Woman-of-the-Bedchamber to the Princess of Wales] and Sir Dighton Probyn [Comptroller and Treasurer to the Prince of Wales] to see the Carringtons at Abergeldie. She is so pretty and nice with her children, but he was rather vulgar.[2]

In the afternoon I was starting out at four for a walk when Florence Lister [wife of Sir Villiers Lister, Lady Glenesk's brother] came, but after showing her the rooms and a little talk she went off and I took a walk up to the Flag Staff and enjoyed it. The Princess of Wales looked lovely at dinner when the Carringtons dined and she is so wise to put even a little help to give her a good colour.

October 13

Glorious day, Lord George left early. I walked with Miss Knollys by the river and round the Hill. At four the Princess of Wales said good-bye so kindly and gave me a beautiful big photo (very like Lady Warwick) of herself, and as I was driving away with the Queen she took a Kodak Photo of the carriage. We went to Braemar and it was bitterly cold

---

[1] The Archbishop was staying with the Gladstones at Hawarden Castle when he died.

[2] The Queen had lent Abergeldie to Lord and Lady Carrington. Charles Robert Wynn-Carrington, 3rd Baron (1843–1928), had been Lord Chamberlain from 1892–1895 when he was created an Earl, and, in 1912, Marquess of Lincolnshire. In 1878 he married the Hon. Celia (Lilly) Harbord, elder daughter of the 5th Baron Suffield. They had five daughters born between 1880 and 1892, and an only son born in 1895. This boy, Viscount Wendover, died of wounds in 1915. On the death of the Marquess, the Earldom and Marquisate became extinct. The surname of the Carringtons had originally been Smith but in 1880 they took the name of Carrington, and in 1896 it was changed again to Wynn-Carrington.

coming back at six, but a lovely sunset with frosty sky. The dinner and evening was nice and quiet and Princess Beatrice talked to me a good deal about a Mr Chambers's book about the life after death, and praying for the dead, which have been a comfort to her.[1] The feeling that the dead are near seems so strong when they are first taken from one.

October 14

Weather warmer and fine. Walked with Ethel Cadogan and her little Mizer in the morning. She is amusing but a dangerous person, and Harriet and she don't get on at all well and irritate each other. In the afternoon drove with the Queen and Harriet. It was rather damp. Only a ladies' dinner with Lady Bigge and the conversation easy and general. The Queen crocheted a little but it is difficult for her to see the stitches. Before dinner the Queen sent me a group with the Emperor and Empress and another of herself and Princess Beatrice. All the gentlemen were in the drawing-room to say good-bye to Sir Fleetwood Edwards.

October 15

I left Balmoral at nine with a little sore throat which rapidly developed into a sort of influenza cold and after a very slow journey and draughty station at Edinburgh, I had a bad face ache and felt so ill on arrival at Bishopsthorpe, York. Dear Augusta Maclagan[2] received me most kindly. I was luckily able to go to a funeral service for the Archbishop of Canterbury on the next day, the 16th, but then nursed myself, and was so heavy and stupid. I left 17th, and as I slept a great deal all day, I arrived better at home but toothache came two days after and lasted about six days (and the nerve killing about two months [later note]). Con went to Ireland,[3] and Ems came down home Monday, 19th, and first told me about Mr Lutyens and his writing to her.

---

[1] *Our Life After Death*, by the Rev. Arthur Chambers, was published in 1894 and had an extraordinary sale.

[2] Lady Lytton's first cousin who had married William Dalrymple Maclagan, Archbishop of York.

[3] To stay with her sister, Betty Balfour. Gerald Balfour had been appointed Chief Secretary for Ireland in 1895.

THE QUEEN WITH THE PRINCE OF WALES,
THE TSAR AND TSARINA AND
THE GRAND-DUCHESS OLGA

[Lady Lytton's youngest daughter, Emily, had been staying at Milford House, Surrey with Mr Robert Webb, squire of Milford, and his wife. Also staying there was Edwin Lutyens who was building a house for Mr Webb, Warren Lodge, near Thursley. Lutyens and Emily fell in love, and after leaving her at Milford to go back to London, he wrote to her in the train on the way to Paddington on October 17 to tell her that he loved her, but adding that he had nothing to offer her but his love. The financial obstacle to their marriage seemed at first insuperable, but after three months their path was smoothed by the wise intervention of Lord Loch who merely required Lutyens to insure his life, and on 30 January 1897 Lady Lytton was able to write in her diary: "Ems was engaged to Ned Lutyens and both were very happy. God bless them and grant them a very happy life together."

The diary continued on February 2 with only one entry:]

I went into waiting at Osborne for a week. The Empress Frederick was there and so lovely and charming and full of interest in all things, and she was so cordial to me the first night after dinner and in her own room one evening. She referred to the unfortunate time in Paris, and was sure it was because Count Münster [the German Ambassador in Paris] made her stay at the Embassy that the French people were angry with her. She thought still that the Emperor Frederick's throat had been irritated by the first German doctor who poked at it with an electric wire, and the thought is very harrowing.

[The Emperor Frederick had died of cancer of the throat on 15 June 1888. When he first complained of a sore throat in January 1887 his physician called into consultation Dr Gerhardt, Professor of Clinical Medicine at the University of Berlin, a specialist in diseases of the throat, who found a nodule on the left vocal cord which he tried to remove with a snare as he was not accustomed to the use of laryngeal forceps. Failing to bring it away, he then made thirteen unsuccessful attempts to burn it away with a galvano-cautery.

The Empress Frederick had three times visited Paris incognito since the Franco-Prussian War, and had always been well received, but in February 1891, at the request of her son, the Kaiser, she paid a semi-official visit, staying at the German Embassy. The Kaiser was anxious to sow the seed of a reconciliation between the two countries, though ostensibly the Empress went to thank those artists who had promised to lend pictures for a forthcoming exhibition in Berlin of which she was the patron.

The first three or four days of the visit went off very well. The Ambassador gave a dinner party each evening in her honour and Lord and Lady Lytton were the principal guests asked to meet her. But then she made the mistake of going to St Cloud to see the ruins of the Palace which had been wantonly destroyed by the Germans in 1870, and to Versailles where her husband had been stationed while the fate of France was being decided. And then, unfortunately, on a visit to the Ministry of Fine Arts, a laurel wreath placed on the monument of Henri Regnault, the painter who had been killed during the war, was removed for fear it might offend her. There was a tremendous outcry against her in the French press, which also accused her of going to see only Jewish art collections, of spending too little money at the antique shops she visited, and of tipping poorly. There may have been some justice in these last accusations, for she was careful with her money, a characteristic inherited from her father, and her Secretary and Chamberlain, Count von Seckendorff, who was responsible for her gratuities, was also known to be parsimonious.

Count von Seckendorff, who had been the head of her Household since 1865, went with her everywhere. While the Emperor was still alive he had been accused by the Empress's enemies in Berlin, after he had angered them by refusing to spy on her, of being her lover, and now it had got about that he and the Empress were secretly married. There seems to be no foundation for this rumour. In her letters the Empress never ceases to bewail her misery and loneliness without her husband, so if she was in love with Seckendorff she was either a great hypocrite, which is hard to believe as it was her very outspokenness and straightforwardness that got her into so much trouble, or it was a very anæmic love. Seckendorff, on the other hand, may well have been in love with her. He remained a bachelor and was absolutely devoted to her for the thirty-six years he was in her service.

The Empress was deeply hurt by the attacks on her at the time of her Paris visit, especially as she was criticised in Germany as well as in France, and she never again took any part in official life. In the spring of 1896 she told Princess Catherine Radziwill that she wondered whether her son had asked her to go to Paris on purpose to discredit her. Evidently the injustice was still rankling when Lady Lytton met her at Osborne six years after the unfortunate visit.]

The Queen looked very well, but it was sad to see her on the 5th in Prince Henry's chapel placing a wreath on the tomb so reverently after a nice little service, and to realise how much sorrow there has been for them all. Prince Drino was brought back from school and was much upset. I only drove with the Queen once, the last day with Fanny Lambart [Maid-of-Honour], and only saw her Majesty to my regret in the evening. Countess Perponcher[1] and Count Seckendorff were very agreeable additions to the English household. Harriet Phipps, Miss Majendie and Fanny Drummond were replaced by Mrs Grant, Ethel Cadogan and Fanny Lambart on the 5th. The weather was delightfully mild and I enjoyed the air and being very warm in the house so much. I told the Queen about my dear Emmie's happiness but she only thought me unselfish to rejoice, and does not care for girls marrying I am told.[2]

[1] The Empress's Lady-in-Waiting, and her constant companion and close friend.
[2] The Queen strongly disapproved also of widows remarrying.

Chapter Four

THE QUEEN had been abroad every spring since 1890. She had been to Biarritz, Aix-les-Bains, Grasse, Hyères and Florence, but in 1895 she went to Cimiez, just above Nice, and continued to go there for the next five years, staying for the first two of them at a small hotel, the Grand, which was said to be very damp, and later at a huge new hotel, built just in front of the Grand and entirely shutting out its view, called in her honour the Excelsior Regina. Mr Cazalet, who had a house at Cimiez, the Villa Liserb[1] (where Princess Beatrice had stayed after the death of Prince Henry), gave her the freedom of his beautiful park adjoining the hotel where she could work in the mornings undisturbed by the curiosity of the hotel guests.

The routine of the Household remained unchanged when the Queen was abroad. Mr Pope-Hennessy in his *Queen Mary* tells us that "every detail of the installation of the Court was carefully supervised, and even the writing-paper was identical in form, quality and printing with that of Windsor Castle or Balmoral, the only difference being the words 'Hotel Regina, Cimiez' beneath the embossed crown. The Queen's drawing-room at the Hotel Regina had red wall-paper, and contained some indifferent pictures lent by an old picture-dealer in Nice. The dining-room next door had a 'vulgar, glaring paper' on which hung copies of the full-length Allan Ramsay coronation portraits of George III and Queen Charlotte." She also took her own bed with her, and her donkey.

At this date the Riviera was so full of royalty of one nationality or another that Lord Salisbury, who had a villa at

---

[1] Liserb spells Bresil backwards, Brazil being the country from which the Cazalet fortune originated. The Villa Liserb no longer exists, and the Parc Liserb has been turned into a housing estate of twenty or thirty villas.

Beaulieu, maintained that it was a choice between royalty in the winter and mosquitoes in the summer.

When the Queen had first gone abroad she had travelled via Boulogne on the ordinary Channel steamer, but now that she was so lame that she could no longer walk, she did not like people seeing her being carried up and down the gangway (there were always crowds waiting to see her on the quay) and therefore she crossed to Boulogne or Cherbourg on the *Victoria and Albert* to ensure a covered gangway. As she took all her Scotch and English servants with her as well as her suite and various members of her family, she travelled with a party of about a hundred. To try to cut down this number, Colonel Carington, one of the Equerries, submitted to her a list of all these servants, thinking she might not realise how many there were, but after going into it carefully she declared that she could not do without one of them.

Although restaurant-cars had been introduced in 1883 by the *Wagon-Lits* company, the Queen did not have one put at her disposal to and from Nice. She was a nervous traveller and no doubt preferred a slower train that stopped for meals. (The restaurant car attached to the Orient Express, which was the prototype of the new rolling stock and appeared in June 1883, cut thirty hours off the journey from Paris to Constantinople.)

In 1897 the Queen left for Cimiez on March 11 and stopped that evening at Noisy-le-Sec on the Ceinture in Paris to meet the French President, M. Félix Faure. He was brought to her railway carriage and presented by Sir Edmund Monson, the British Ambassador. She received him alone and they discussed the unhappy situation which had arisen over Crete. The island had for many years formed part of the Ottoman Empire but as the population was mainly Greek and Christian there was much unrest. In February an insurrection had broken out and an appeal had been made to Greece to help free the country from Turkish domination. Feeling in Greece was so strongly in sympathy with the insurgents that King George had been forced to send troops to the island. The Sultan, urged by the Great Powers, had agreed to grant autonomy to Crete under Turkish suzerainty on condition that Greece immediately withdrew her troops; but this Greece had refused to do. As King George of Greece was a brother of the Princess of Wales, and as Sophie, the Empress Frederick's daughter, was married to the Greek Crown Prince, the Prince and Princess of Wales as well as the Empress Frederick were putting tremendous pressure on the Queen to side actively with Greece; but although she was very sorry for the Greek Royal family, the Queen's true sympathies were with the Sultan, and she was endeavouring to ease the situation by diplomacy. In spite of all the efforts of the Great Powers, however, Turkey declared war on Greece on April 17 and invaded Thessaly. The Greeks were quickly beaten and forced to sue for peace. There was little real fighting.

Among those travelling with the Queen to Cimiez that winter were Princess Beatrice and her children and Princess Helena Victoria of Schleswig-Holstein. This Princess, who was known as Thora in the family, was constantly with her grandmother. She was going to be twenty-seven in May and according to *Country Life* had "refused some excellent offers of marriage rather than leave England." When one remembers that the Queen did "not care for girls marrying" one cannot help wondering whether it was because of her great attachment to this particular grand-daughter that Thora never found a husband.

In April Lady Lytton went out to join the Queen. It must have been very painful for her to go to Cimiez because she and her husband had been there together the year before his death. She left England on April 9, having spent the night in London, and travelled over to Paris with her son, Victor, by way of Newhaven and Dieppe. On the journey she began reading *Carnets de Voyage*, a posthumous book by Taine who had died in 1893, which she found "so well written." Her younger son, Neville, who had now left Eton and was studying art in Paris under Léon Bonnat, the portrait painter,[1] met them at the Gare St Lazare "looking a tower of strength and so cheery, and he and I sat on luxurious

---

[1] It was Neville's father who had decided that he was to be an artist. He had arranged before his death that Neville should study in Paris under Bonnat.

chairs, put for the purpose outside the station for travellers waiting. How civilised."

Her diary continued:

Saturday, April 10

In Paris I shopped in the morning and in the afternoon called at the Embassy, and found Lady Monson pretty and very cordial and so was he, coming in on purpose to talk to me so kindly. The dear rooms are so changed with so much "le Mapel,"[1] as it is called, furniture, screens and pictures, one can hardly move, and I felt in a dream that made me sick. From there I went to Neville's rooms, 22 rue Dufrénoy, to see his studies which are very clever, and Bonnat told Sir E. Monson that Neville was developing a great deal of talent. The dear sons dined with me at seven and we went to see *La Loi de l'Homme* by Hervieu at the *Français*, an interesting play, and though the situations are painful they are dramatic, and Bartet acted so well, and far more passion since her great sorrow losing her son.

Palm Sunday morning, April 11

Dear Nev asked me to stay for the Sacrament, and Vic stayed also though the stuffy church tried him so much. Several came to see us during our Hotel luncheon, Lady Finlay and Will, Austin Lee[2] and Alick Yorke, whom I was anxious to thank for his great kindness in lending us his rooms in London [32a Orchard Street]. He wore an enormous Malmaison Carnation in his button hole. I said after to Lee, "Are button holes worn now?" "Well not the peony size of Alick's," he answered. Lee would have gone out with us, and Alick returned in a Brougham most kindly to offer me a drive, but the sons and I clung to each other, and walked in the Tuileries and Champs Élysées full of happy merry parents

[1] Maple had opened a branch in Paris in 1888.

[2] Austin Lee had been Lord Lytton's Private Secretary in Paris. He was still attached to the British Embassy. Lady Finlay was the daughter of Cosmo Innes, Advocate of Edinburgh, and the wife of Sir Robert Finlay, Solicitor General 1895–1900. Will was their only son, born 1875, who became a judge and succeeded as 2nd Viscount Finlay. His father was created a Viscount in 1919, but the peerage became extinct at Will's death in 1945.

7

and children. Nevs would roar with laughter over the ball game, I had to restrain him. When I got tired the dear ones went on the Boulevards alone, and I prepared myself for the journey. After dinner Vic and Nevs came to the Gare de Lyon and started me at the abominably served Gare du Midi, everyone indifferent, and the difficulty to get served with tickets, luggage weighed etc. rather puzzling, but Vic walks and talks like a man in authority and there was plenty of time, so all went well and I was lodged in the stuffy compartment of the train *de luxe* (?) with stuffy passages and vulgar men walking about. The *Coupés lits* are really the best, except that the *carrèage* [*sic*] is not so steady so one does not sleep so sound. At six I got up to wash myself before anyone was about, and, Oh, horror when I returned to the silent passage I had no clue where Checketts my maid was, and which was my compartment, but judging about right, I only opened one wrong, and then was relieved to find my own place. At Avignon where I had some coffee brought in, Checketts felt sick and could not take any, and from there the scenery was so lovely getting every minute more Southern with lilacs and other blossoms, and the sky blue and the morning lights with true sunshine so entrancing. The approach to Marseilles is also always lovely and the peeps of Mediterranean blue seas, and all along to Nice the colouring was lovely and rose gardens so luxuriant. The *déjeuner* at Toulon served abominably but I got a little at a side table.

The Courier, Dossé,[1] met us so I could drive off at once and the sunshine was so brilliant, but the huge Palace white Hotel Regina an insult to dear old Cimiez.[2] All were very kind in receiving me, and I had some luncheon about three quietly in Mr Fritz Ponsonby's room, and Colonel Carington

[1] E. Dossé was, on 10 May 1890, appointed "Director of Her Majesty's Continental journeys," presumably succeeding the famous courier Kanné, who had died in April 1888, having attended the Queen on all her Continental journeys since 1857.

[2] This hotel, still bearing the name Regina and still painted white, has now been turned into expensive unfurnished flats. At the bottom of the well-kept garden is a statue of Queen Victoria by Maubert put up in 1912. The Grand Hotel, just behind the Regina, is now an old people's home and bears on its gate a plaque stating that Queen Victoria stayed there in the spring of 1895 and 1896.

came to see me, and I just said good-bye to Lady Antrim [Lady-in-Waiting], who was hurrying off. Harriet Phipps advised me to go to bed, and I supposed it was the best chance for the evening, but I was sleeping so soundly at eight it was hard to get up.

The Austrian Archduchess Sophie(?) widow of the Crown Prince dined and it was interesting to see her, who had gone through so much.[1] The Queen saw me as she was coming out of her room before coming into the drawing-room. The Queen's rooms and all are certainly most comfortable and beautifully furnished in this hotel, and the cooking, a mixture of one of the Queen's cooks and one of the hotel, was really excellent.

The time from Monday 12th to Wednesday 28th passed most pleasantly, only I had too many hours of restless waiting in my own bedroom, where I sat as I disturbed no one as in the sitting-rooms, and my bedroom was very large and I screened off the bed and washing stand. I had my coffee in my room but did not go out till past twelve when the Queen was out, and yet I am never wanted in the mornings. The drives with the Queen, about every other day, were delightful up in the mountains and having tea at the side of the road brought to the carriage. On Good Friday after the Service in the Chapel arranged for the Queen in the hotel, I was going out and met Princess Victoria [Thora] who asked me to walk with her and we went in to the Cimiez Convent Church [a Franciscan monastery]. All Nice was very quiet, and reverence for the day shown as in Paris. Easter Eve I felt faint at dinner, and though sitting by the Queen had to

[1] She meant the Archduchess, or rather the Crown Princess, Stéphanie, daughter of Leopold II of Belgium. In 1881 Stéphanie had married the Crown Prince Rudolph who shot himself at Mayerling in 1889. She was still only thirty-one in 1897. The Archduchess Sophie had been Rudolph's grandmother. She had never become Empress because her husband, Franz Charles, in order to save the Hapsburg dynasty, had renounced his right to the throne in favour of their son, Franz Joseph. In 1900 Princess Stéphanie married Elemér, Count Lónyay de Nagy-Lónya, whom she had first met in the autumn of 1896 while on a visit to the Isle of Wight. It was a love match in which she found happiness at last, but her parents never forgave her for making such a low marriage. The Emperor Franz Joseph, however, gave her his full support and a generous allowance.

ask to be excused, but I came back in the evening for the guests. Captain Sir Henry and Lady Pooer of the *Hawk* ship at Villefranche came, and the Queen told us after she was so vexed as her maid looking out the names in the Baronetage told her wrong that he had a first wife and children, but on questioning found this was wrong, and yet the Queen laughed over it.

[It was Sir Richard Poore, 4th Baronet, not Sir Henry Pooer, who was Captain of the *Hawk*. In 1885 he had married Ida Margaret, daughter of the Rev. Charles Graves. He and his wife dined with the Queen on April 15, the day before Good Friday. He was sailing for Crete on the 28th. The Queen's maid could not have mixed him up with his father, Sir Edward, whom he succeeded in 1893, because Sir Edward had been married only once. There was no other knight or baronet of that name, or anything approaching that name, so the maid no doubt looked up the Marquess of Waterford whose family name is De La Poer Beresford. Henry De La Poer, though he had succeeded in 1895, had only married in 1897 so he would not have been in the Baronetage as a married man, whereas his father, John Henry, had been married twice and had had two families. The Queen in her journal makes no allusion to the mistake.]

Easter Sunday [April 18] I was ill from 5 a.m., when the Convent Bells were ringing for the feast, from Colic but just went to the Service and then excused myself and went to bed till dinner time when I was able to be up and eat something.

When driving the Queen will sometimes talk of political affairs and she blamed Austria and Germany for not joining properly the concert of Europe, and she is very sorry for the Greeks but when they showed but little fight in them and the Turkish Army behaved so well, the Queen spoke of it most justly. The Queen also mentioned one day that a French journalist had wanted to write of the Queen's favourites. "As if I had had any," she answered. So it was changed to the Queen's friends, and then it was all put wrong and some people mentioned she hardly knew or did not care for, and it was all very disagreeable. Princess Victoria told us one day a man had written suggesting that a puppet Queen should be in the carriage for the Jubilee Procession [to take place on June 22] to save the Queen from fatigue. It reminded me of *King Poppy*, dear Robert's poem.[1]

The drives to La Tourette, Aspremont, the old Corniche road (where we met Lady Salisbury and party who all looked shy when the Queen stopped to speak to them). The Queen says she likes the foreign easy manner but our Royal circle does not inspire it as Princess Beatrice is very shy and the Queen does not like people to talk loud or be at all wanting in reverence and loyalty which is alarming (and yet pushing people are much received at Court).

Easter Monday there were lovely fireworks and the garden illuminated with little oil lamps looked so well, but it was very chilly even with fur coats on the balcony.

The 19th of April the Queen wore a bunch of primroses and there were lovely ones sent from Windsor in all our rooms. The 20th I drove with the Queen and Princess Beatrice to Cap Martin. The sun was quite hot and the Queen got a little tired before we arrived but bore it very well. The road reminded me of dear Robert all the way in his grey coat as we drove to Monte Carlo in 1890 together, but I loved the beauty and thoughts of him, though I could hardly keep back my tears. The flowers all the way were exquisite. The Empress Eugénie looks much aged and hard in the face but received the Queen very gracefully. Her Villa is charming and in perfect taste though rather empty.[2] We lunched only with the old lady, and then walked in the garden, which was quite lovely, with only a few planted shrubs mixing in with

[1] Lord Lytton's long allegorical poem, *King Poppy*, which he began in 1875 and almost entirely rewrote at Cimiez in 1890, was not published until after his death. To save King Poppy's daughter from a prophesied fate, a lifelike puppet was constructed to take her place at all court functions.

[2] The Empress Eugénie had bought this estate at Cap Martin early in the nineties. Her villa, which she called Cyrnos in memory of the Bonapartes (Cyrnos being the Greek name for Corsica), bears the date 1893. It is on the west slope of Cap Martin, with the garden going down to the sea, and is still privately owned.

the wildness down to the sea through the pines, and Monaco
in the distance. The roses everywhere hung in such luxuriance
and beauty. The Empress was kept a long time at the door
before we drove off. On passing the Château Malet the Queen
drove up and had some tea at the entrance where the Malets,
Duke of Bedford and his small son,[1] and Lady Galloway
[Lord Salisbury's half-sister] came up. Princess Beatrice got
out, but I did not like to leave the Queen. The inside of the
Villa is done up with great vulgarity all said, and not in good
taste.

One morning I was looking out of the window and I saw
a gushing lady run up and embrace the head of the Queen's
donkey, not being able to approach her Majesty any nearer.
The Coachman looked solemn and soon led away the
donkey and chair.[2] The 21st, the Rivolis (Duc and Duchesse)
with their daughters beautifully coiffé'd came to dinner and
they were so well dressed in mourning for Madame Heine
her mother. Baron Reuter came in the evening to be presented,
but the Queen was very shy and did not say much. He has the
Jewish face most marked and a tiny figure. He is very civil
in supplying the Queen with telegrams but not without
payment.[3]

After a quiet day on the 22nd Sarah Bernhardt gave a
lovely little piece, in the drawing-room before the Queen,
Jean Marie by A. Theuriet, and she acted it with the greatest
feeling and her voice was lovely. The story like *Robin Gray*.[4]
It had been Sarah's great wish to act before the Queen, and
when I called her up at the end to present her, the tears were
rolling down her cheeks with emotion. There were also

[1] The Château Malet, Monte Carlo, belonged to Sir Edward and Lady
Ermyntrude Malet. She was a daughter of the 9th Duke of Bedford. It was
Lady Ermyntrude's brother who was staying at the Château Malet. His
"small son" had been born in December 1888. His mother, the Dowager
Duchess, who had been the Queen's Mistress of the Robes, died on April 23.

[2] The Queen's donkey was pure white and had been brought for her from
Egypt by Lord Wolseley. In July 1899 Lord Kitchener was entrusted with
the task of finding "the finest female white donkey procurable in Egypt" as a
mate for it.

[3] Baron de Reuter was at this time eighty-one. Although he had in 1878
handed over control of Reuters to his elder son, Herbert, he remained on the
Board of Directors up to the day of his death, 25 February 1899.

[4] Ballad of *Auld Robin Gray* by Lady Anne Lindsay (1750–1825).

the two men. I had a word with Sarah before the Queen came in, about Paris days, and altogether it was quite upsetting to me. The Queen after spoke of the pleasure it had been, and I told the stories of Sarah's goodness to fellow artists and getting the gold medal for attending to the wounded under fire after the war in France, and all I could say for her.

[It is rather surprising that Lady Lytton should have been such a friend of Sarah Bernhardt, seeing how bad was Sarah's moral reputation, but Lord Lytton had been a great admirer of hers, and Lady Lytton was guided in all things by his judgement. So much so indeed that after his death she wanted to see only those people whom he had loved, even though she may have been jealous of them in his lifetime.

The Queen wrote in her journal on April 22: "At half past six the famous and celebrated actress Sarah Bernhardt, who had been acting at Nice and is staying in this hotel, performed a little piece for us in the drawing-room at her own request. The play was called *Jean Marie*, by Adrien Fleuriet,[1] quite short, only lasting half an hour. It is extremely touching, and Sarah Bernhardt's acting was quite marvellous, so pathetic and full of feeling. She appeared much affected herself, tears rolling down her cheeks. She has a most beautiful voice, and is very graceful in all her movements. The story is much the same as that of *Auld Robin Gray*. The two who acted with her were also excellent, particularly the one who took the part of Jean Marie. When the play was over, Edith L. presented Sarah Bernhardt to me, and I spoke to her for a few moments. Her manner was most pleasing and gentle. She said it had been such a pleasure and honour to act for me. When I expressed the hope that she was not tired, she answered, 'Cela m'a reposée.' "

The Queen had at first been reluctant to allow Sarah Bernhardt to appear before her and one likes to think that it was Lady Lytton who persuaded her to give herself this pleasure. Certainly it was a triumph, for the general opinion of her among "ladies" was expressed by the Empress

---

[1]The author was in fact André Theuriet. The mistake in the published journal is evidently an error of transcription.

Frederick in a letter to her daughter Sophie in 1893: "It must have been interesting to see Sarah Bernhardt, she is an extraordinary actress from all I have heard. I hope you did *not* make her acquaintance, as alas no *lady* can, she is so very bad, and has an awful reputation. It is a pity those immoral pieces are always given, such as those you saw." We are not told what these immoral pieces were.

But the honour for Sarah Bernhardt of appearing before the Queen was rather diminished by its aftermath which Frederick Ponsonby recounts in his *Recollections of Three Reigns:*

"The Queen was very particular about people writing their names in her Birthday Book. She took the last volume of this about with her everywhere she went and on occasion it had been mistaken for the Bible. . . . When the Queen was abroad one of the Equerries was responsible for this most tiresome book." Ponsonby was in charge of the book that year at Cimiez, and at the end of Sarah Bernhardt's performance: "I instinctively felt this was a case for the Birthday Book, and after the Queen had left the drawing-room I produced the book and asked Sarah Bernhardt to write her name. She startled me by insisting on kneeling down on the floor to write. Then she took up nearly the whole of one page by writing 'Le plus beau jour de ma vie' and signed it with a flourish.

"I felt I had done my duty nobly and when a message came from the Queen asking me whether I had got Sarah Bernhardt's signature I sent the book in with pride for the Queen to see. To my surprise I got no marks. First of all it was the wrong book, and I ought to have used the artists' book, and secondly I ought to have prevented her from taking up the whole page. I was told the Queen was much put out at this, but in any case I was to get Sarah Bernhardt's signature in the artists' book. By the merest chance I heard she was leaving Nice for Marseilles that night after the performance in the theatre, so there was only one thing to do, and that was to catch her before she left; but this was not as easy as I imagined, as I found out she never saw anyone before going to the theatre. I therefore had an early dinner and took a stall for *La Tosca*. After the first act I went round to the box-office and said I wished to see Madame Sarah Bernhardt, but the man, who no doubt had often to grapple with many others who had the same wish, replied with a pitying smile that it was hopeless to try and see her and hinted that I had better fasten my affection on someone else. It was impossible to argue with a busy man who kept on being interrupted and so I contented myself with asking to see her secretary, and after some trouble he said he would arrange this.

"As soon as the next *entr'acte* began I returned to the box-office and after an interminable delay the secretary came, and although polite was very short in his answers. So I had to play the Queen and said, 'Je viens de la part de Sa Majesté La Reine d'Angleterre.' He at once was all over the place and took me to the back of the theatre, where I found in a sort of antechamber a lot of people waiting to see Sarah. But the Queen's name worked like a talisman, and I was taken at once to her dressing-room, where she received me most cordially. There were two dressers, two sort of ladies-in-waiting, the secretary, and another whom I took to be the lover. I explained my errand, and she said in her *voix d'or*, 'Je l'ai déjà ecrit,' I replied that this was so, but I had been commanded to obtain her signature in another book, and I murmured something about its being 'plus intime.' She said certainly she would write, but although the whole party looked everywhere, there was no ink. The lover did find a property inkstand and an old split quill, but no ink. There was nothing to do but to come back during the next *entr'acte*, and the secretary was told to get busy and procure some ink and a pen. Accordingly I sat through the next act and returned, not without difficulty, to her dressing-room. The ink and pen were produced and Sarah wrote her name, but of course there was no blotting-paper. I was so anxious that she should not see the other signatures that as soon as she had written I tried to take away the book. 'Un moment que ca sèche,' she said, and before I could stop her she glanced at the other signatures where several well-known artists' names appeared. The spell was broken. She handed back the book to me with a shrug of the shoulders. She understood."]

Another evening the Bishop of Gibraltar[1] (very stiff and dull) and Lord Rowton [Montagu Curry] dined, and the Clergyman and his wife [Mr and Mrs Langford] and the doctor and his dame [Dr and Mrs Sturge who lived in Nice] in the evening. It was very dull, but I did my best to be civil and then heard the Queen did not like one's going on talking after she had left, but no one ever helps one to do what is wanted of one, and it is so paralysing and makes me so cross with H [Harriet Phipps] who might help when all is new to one.

Even on the 23rd of April there was the most irritating wind and fine white dust and the town so trying. I went with Princess Beatrice shopping in the morning and for a drive in the afternoon and I could hardly see in the evening, but there were only ladies, those nice dinners when the Queen and Princesses talk so easily and well.

The 24th April it rained and was milder, and after one I got a turn when not wanted. Princess Beatrice gave me a little parasol from the Queen after luncheon very shyly saying, "Mama thought you would like this," and then turned away.

After the ladies had gone to Monte Carlo I drove to see Lady Salisbury at La Bastide. She seemed very low, and alarmingly large from the dropsy and Gwenny thanked me for coming. (An operation was performed on her return to England which gave great relief, but how long will it last?)[2] Lady Salisbury told me of a battle and complete defeat of the Greeks by the Turks and now I hope there may be no more fighting. The garden round the Bastide, the Salisburys' place, is growing up and very pretty marguerites and some flowers, but it still looks new. The drive back was quite cold but nice without dust after the rain.

[1] The Rt. Rev. Charles Waldegrave Sandford (1828–1903). He retired to a house at Cannes which he called Bishopsbourne. He had been Rector of Bishopsbourne, Kent, 1870–74.

[2] A later note in Lady Lytton's writing. Lady Salisbury had been very ill and had been recuperating at La Bastide, Beaulieu, for over two months. Her unmarried daughter, Lady Gwendoline Cecil, was with her. The villa, set high above Beaulieu with a wonderful view and a hillside garden of several acres, was left to Lady Gwendoline who sold it in 1914. It has now been turned into unfurnished flats.

Sunday, April 25

Lovely hot day. After the Service in the Chapel I walked to Mrs Evans and she picked me a glorious lot of roses, carnations and masses of flowers and I walked back so proud of my gorgeous basket.¹ I kept a few and sent the rest to Sir Charles Cust [Equerry to the Duke of York], who has been going through seven weeks of typhoid fever. Mrs Evans sent the Queen a glorious lot of roses the next day and the table was decorated with them for dinner. Mrs Evans and Mrs Wagstaff were so nice to me. The Sunday afternoon I drove alone with the Queen and one of the young Battenberg Princes to Notre Dame? up the Var Valley, a sacred place where are some healing waters and we met in an uncomfortably narrow road a lot of pilgrims returning.² We had tea very cheerily just below the church, but it got quite chilly. Prince Leopold [Princess Beatrice's second son, aged seven] gave the Queen a little medal for luck from the church, which she seemed to care for much. At dinner the Queen told me of the birth of the Duchess of York's little girl on the anniversary of Princess Alice's birth. And being Jubilee year it was said the names must be Victoria Alice.³ In the evening we had a cheery ladies' dinner and some music. Princess Beatrice plays well and Miss Bulteel [Lady-in-Waiting to Princess Beatrice] also.

¹ I have not been able to identify Mrs Evans, but on 31 March 1896 the Queen wrote in her journal at Cimiez: "Went a little down the old road, round to the Villa del Torre di Cimella, belonging to an old English lady, Mrs Evans, who has lately lost her husband. The garden is perfectly beautiful, and the house a fine one, which would have done very well for me, but she cannot spare it, as she requires to go there all the winter, for her health. She built the house and laid out the garden entirely herself. She came out to speak to us." (Unpublished extract.)

² Lady Lytton has made a mistake here. The church they went to that day was not in the Var Valley. It was Notre Dame de Laghet, and though there are no healing waters there, it claims to be the most celebrated place of pilgrimage in the Alpes-Maritimes. Laghet is a hamlet near La Turbie. Queen Victoria visited Notre Dame de Laghet on April 21 as well as on the 25th, both these visits being recorded in the museum of the sanctuary.

³ Princess Mary (now the Princess Royal) was christened Victoria Alexandra Alice Mary at Sandringham on Whit Monday, June 7. The Queen commented in her Journal: "It is strange that this child should be born on dear Alice's birthday, whilst the last was on the anniversary of her death."

Monday, April 26

I went to the town for the Queen, to give the General's wife[1] a jewelled cypher brooch and she seemed so pleased.

The 27th, very hot but got a nice drive to St Antoine late. Ladies' dinner but Princess Beatrice rather cross to the Queen about the game of Halma having been given up, and Princess Beatrice said she had given up so much, which is no doubt true. I went on the balcony in low dress without chill.

April 28

This is our last evening but we have had three lovely days and such masses of roses keep pouring in, but they say it is of no use to try to take them to England.

April 29

The storm yesterday from Nice was most lucky. The night had been so hot, but then came a lovely good rain, which just ceased for our drive down to the station, so there was no dust as might have been, with the mounted escort. The household followed the Queen in two carriages. The streets were thinly lined with people, who looked like visitors through Nice and the Queen got lovely bouquets. It was not at all hot in the train even on starting. Miss Phipps and I are in one carriage together. We had luncheon from a big basket in the train. The colouring was not pretty for the scenery, but absence of dust was so perfect. The day passed off very well. Tea was given in at another station and we got out for dinner and waited an hour, and then Miss Phipps went to the Queen's carriage and I got to bed comfortably. The night seemed eternally long, but I got up at six to see the environs of Paris and it is all lovely and bright and the spring leaves and blossoms very perfect. Later there was a heavy fog over dear Paris at 8.15. I did wish I could see Nevs.

[1] Mme Gebhardt. General Gebhardt was the Governor of Nice. The Gebhardts had dined with the Queen on April 24 and "were full of kind expressions about our stay and approaching departure." (Unpublished extract from the Queen's journal.)

On board Queen's yacht. April 29. All went well till Cherbourg. The Queen looked flushed as she got out after the
twenty-eight hours but at the pleasant ladies' dinner she
talked easily and wondered why the Princesses did not feel
inclined to write till 1 a.m.

I got a walk in the town with Colonel Carington to take
care of me, as it is not always easy to get back into the Dock
Yard. The sea is as calm as a mill-pond which anyhow is
comforting for the night, but the noise on the yacht prevented
my sleeping after four but my cabin is so nice and large.

6 p.m. in train going to Windsor. Just passed Milford in
sunshine! Had a most enjoyable day, sitting on deck till two
and leaving Cherbourg all looked so pretty, slowly steaming
away with the band playing dear English tunes, and passing
great ugly grey French warships and such lovely sunshine
and blue sea and our four ships accompanying. The yacht is so
smart and all the officers also. The Princesses and young
Princes came on deck also. After a good luncheon the weather
became thick and wet and for a moment the Admiral
[Fullerton] seemed very anxious and could not tell where he
was, but once the light-ship came in sight it was all right and
his precious charge brought safely to land by 4.15. The land-
ing-stage at Portsmouth was not nearly so pretty as the
French one.

We got to Windsor about half past seven and, Oh, so
cold. Another nice ladies' dinner and only Harriet and myself.
Princess Beatrice said she could not bear Poetry and the
Queen said: "Oh, I like it very much." I asked, "Which was
your favourite poet, Mam?" "Oh, certainly Scott," the
Queen answered, and in her youth the excitement over his
writing must have been great so one can understand it, for
it is the favourite poet of our youth we always remember.

I left Windsor early the morning of the 2nd of May, and
went home with dear Ems and Ned.

[Lady Lytton was not in waiting on the Queen for her
Diamond Jubilee. June 20 happened to fall on a Sunday and
thanksgiving services were held throught the Empire. On the

22nd, the Jubilee was celebrated "with enthusiasm, splendour and accord," as the Annual Register described it. The crowds were enormous and for four nights no traffic was allowed in the principal streets. The Queen drove in state for three hours through six miles of London streets, going from Buckingham Palace to St Paul's north of the river, and coming back by way of London Bridge and a route south of the river.[1] At St Paul's Cathedral she stopped at the steps but did not get out of her carriage, and a short service was held and the Te Deum sung in the open air. At her own request the only reigning Sovereign who came over for the Jubilee was her cousin, the King of the Belgians with his youngest daughter Princess Clementina. She did not feel up to entertaining kings, but riding in her procession were Colonial and Indian troops and the Prime Ministers of all the self-governing colonies, all her sons and daughters and as many of her grandchildren as possible. She had wanted all the Indian Princes to be there too, but most of them were kept at home coping with the terrible plague and famine which had swept over India that year.

The evening before the procession there had been a banquet at Buckingham Palace and for the first time in her widowhood the Queen, persuaded by the Princess of Wales, went out of black. She herself described in her journal what she wore: " a dress of which the whole front was embroidered in gold, which had been specially worked in India, diamonds in my cap and a diamond necklace, etc."

For her procession she wore "a dress of black silk, trimmed with panels of grey satin veiled with black net and steel embroideries, and some black lace, my lovely diamond chain given me by my younger children, round my neck. My bonnet was trimmed with creamy white flowers and white aigrette and some black lace."

Congratulations and presents came from all over the world, and festivities and receptions of various kinds and the

[1] The Queen drove in an open carriage as the weather was perfect, and held up a very long-handled black lace parasol lined with white, given to her for the occasion by Lady Lytton's uncle, Charles Villiers, who was known as "Father of the House of Commons," having been the member for Wolverhampton since 1835. He was born in 1802 and died in 1898.

presentation of addresses were still going on when Lady
Lytton went to Windsor in July.]

Saturday, July 3

Left home early so as to see Wally Paget[1] in London,
she was amusing as usual and told me of the cure in Germany
where Gay was, for chilliness and indigestion. You sit half
the day with very little clothing on.

I got down to Windsor for tea and Vic [both her sons were
on a visit to Eton] joined me in the sitting-room and we went
out together as allowed and saw the end of the garden party
for the House of Commons and it was very well done with
large tents filled with flowers and refreshment and even
cigars left for all to take who liked, and everyone seemed
happy. Vic and I enjoyed walking round together and on such
a lovely evening, then he went back to Eton and I to my
lady-in-waiting rooms in the Castle. A quiet evening so I
could talk to the Queen and she seemed pleased with the
reception in the afternoon.[2]

Sunday, July 4

So pleased to hear Elwin [Rector of Booton in Norfolk]
was coming to marry Ems and Ned in August. Dear sons
came with me to St George's and walk after in the grounds
but it was chilly. Duke and Duchess of Edinburgh and Mrs
Monson [Lady-in-Waiting to the Duchess of Edinburgh]
at dinner.

July 5

Very warm which I do so enjoy. Went in the morning to
the Frogmore gardens and saw a new flower in the House
like a small arum, and yellow. I begged for some cut flowers

[1] Walburga, widow of Sir Augustus Paget who had died the year before.
Their daugher, Gay, had married in 1883 Robert Windsor-Clive, created Earl
of Plymouth in 1905.
[2] The reception of the House of Commons at Buckingham Palace on June 23
had been so badly managed that many of the Members did not get into the
Throne-room. To make up, the Queen gave a garden-party for Members and
their wives at Windsor on July 3. This was a great success.

which were sent up. Pertab Singh[1] and two other Indians and a European gentleman lunched with us, then the Queen received forty of the Indian Escort in the Park, and they bowed so well especially Pertab Singh. At 6.15 I went to Frogmore and drove with Princess Louis of Battenberg in a second carriage to Beaumont College,[2] where the Queen received an address and the boy read it perfectly and the cheers were all given together so well. The Queen was given a lovely bouquet of orchids, and then we drove on, but the dust was trying. The Princess was charming and talked so easily. We had a ladies' dinner, six of us altogether and then talk is always easy. Sir Arthur Sullivan was just brought in in the evening, for a five minutes' talk and received the medal. The Poet Laureate [Alfred Austin] was received in the same way I believe the week before.

[Arthur Sullivan was a friend of many members of the Royal family, especially of the Tecks and of the Prince and Princess of Wales. On 1 April 1897 he had written from Villefranche, where he was staying, to the Prince of Wales asking whether he might receive the Queen's command to compose something special for the Jubilee. He pointed out that he had made his career during her Majesty's reign and that his life's work had been so directed that when the musical history of the reign was chronicled his name should not be left out. He suggested that his work should take the form of a hymn-tune to be sung at the service at St Paul's to the accompaniment of a military band. The Queen granted his request and he played the harmonium to her at the chapel in the hotel at Cimiez and received from her "a lovely pocket book" as a souvenir of the occasion. There was some discussion as to who should write the words for the hymn, Sullivan refusing to set to music Alfred Austin's Jubilee poem, and in the end the Bishop of Wakefield, Walsham How (who died later that year), wrote the words, and the "pretty

[1] Lieut.-Colonel Dhiraj Sir Pertab Singh (1845–1920); A.D.C. to the Prince of Wales; Regent of Jodhpur; Maharaja of Idar 1901–1911. He was a great polo player.

[2] Roman Catholic Boys' School at Old Windsor, founded in 1861. Princess Louis was the grandmother of the present Duke of Edinburgh.

and appropriate" hymn, as the Queen called it in her journal, was sung before her on June 20, not at St Paul's, but at St George's Chapel, Windsor, and at churches throughout the Empire. According to his biographer, Hesketh Pearson, Sullivan's "reward came on July 5 when he had dinner with the Household at Windsor, twenty minutes' conversation with the Queen in the long corridor and the gift of the Jubilee medal," but according to Lady Lytton he was given only "a five minutes' talk."]

July 6

Quiet day. Drove with Harriet to call at Lady Southampton's nice house [Winkfield Lodge, Windsor]. The Duke and Duchess of Portland [he was Master of the Horse] and Grand Duke and Duchess of Hesse were at dinner [he was the brother of the Tsarina].

July 7

Large luncheon in St George's Hall. Duke of Devonshire [Lord President of the Council] presided and I sat between him and Mr [Sir James] Reid, and all the Colonial people and wives were there which was very interesting and the Queen received them after luncheon. Mr and Mrs Chamberlain were also there.[1] Lord and Lady Cadogan [he was Lord Lieutenant of Ireland], the Hugh Wyndhams [he was Minister at Bucharest], Arthur Balfour [First Lord of the Treasury] and Prince [Victor] Duleep Singh were at dinner, and there was a lot of standing but it was amusing.

July 8

The Cadogans and Wyndhams were at breakfast and then left. I went to Eton to see Mrs Parry [her sons' Dame] at twelve. There was a large luncheon of a hundred and thirty before receiving deputations at a Court in the large Tapestry

[1] Joseph Chamberlain, the Colonial Secretary, had in 1888 married as his third wife Mary, only daughter of William Crowninship Endicott, American judge and statesman. She became Mrs Carnegie after his death and was over ninety when she died in 1957.

room. The Church came first and the Archbishop of Canterbury [Frederick Temple] read his address very well. The
Queen's voice was beautiful when thanking. I went down to
wait at Frogmore and then drove with the Queen and
Princess Beatrice.

[The Queen had received a hundred Bishops who had
come to England to attend a pan-Anglican Conference at
Lambeth in commemoration of the 1300th anniversary of
the conversion of Britain to Christianity. Princess Marie
Louise in her memoirs writes about this occasion: "Her
Majesty was at Windsor, and had had an exhausting reception of both the houses of Convocation as well as the various
bishops and ecclesiastical dignitaries from overseas. When it
was all over she went for her usual afternoon drive. Edith,
Lady Lytton, was in waiting and accompanied her. There
was rather a prolonged silence at first, and then the Queen
said, 'A very ugly party.' Of course, black shovel hats, black
gaiters, black silk aprons, and the whole rather gloomy
tailoring of these worthy divines was a striking contrast to
the gorgeous and colourful Indian and Eastern guests she
had been entertaining. Then after a further pause, 'I do not
like bishops.' Edith Lytton nearly fell out of the carriage in
surprise and horror. 'Oh, but your dear Majesty likes *some*
bishops . . .'
   " 'Yes,' said her gracious Majesty, 'I like the man but
not the bishop!'
   "I presume the drive, in Edith's opinion, was rather
shattering."
   Lady Lytton unfortunately tells us nothing of this conversation, and one wonders whether Princess Marie Louise
had an account of it from her or from Princess Beatrice or
from the Queen herself. If the Queen did make such remarks
about bishops it is difficult to imagine Lady Lytton being
so very horrified.]

July 9
   Went to call at the Deanery which is such an interesting
old house. I saw the old cloister at the back where Henry

VIII saw Anne Boleyn walking and fell in love with her,[1] and I went through to the Albert Memorial Chapel. After lunch the Queen received the old Crimean nurses and I had to present them. They went out with Miss Florence Nightingale who is still alive but an invalid.[2] Augusta Maclagan and her girl Dorothy [who came out the following year and never married] came and I took them over the Castle which is very tiring though the rooms with the lovely Pictures and the Library I always enjoy. I drove to see Mrs Carington [American wife of Colonel Carington] whose place is very nice.

Duke of Norfolk [Postmaster General] and two Rajahs, Kapurthala and Thakore of Morvi dined and I had to bring them up in the evening. They speak English fluently but are not reverent enough to the Queen, standing with arms akimbo and leaning on her table. I can't believe receiving the Rajahs so privately is a good thing. [Kapurthala was created K.C.S.I. at the Jubilee, and Morvi G.C.S.I.] Sir Julian and Lady Pauncefote [he was Ambassador at Washington] also dined. I sat by the Duke of Norfolk who told me all about his little son.[3]

July 10

Guests at breakfast but the Rajahs came late, and were taken out after with carriages and four horses and the Queen was very particular that they should have every attention. I sat out on the Terrace and it was so hot. Aline Majendie and Mary Hughes[4] were busy with Princess Beatrice. Large luncheon, thirty people before another Court. Lady Sophie Palmer brought her nephews and Wang and all had

[1] This story, though widely known and believed, lacks any historical foundation.

[2] She died in 1910 at the age of ninety.

[3] By his first marriage in 1877 to Lady Flora Hastings the Duke of Norfolk had had a son, Philip Joseph Mary, born in 1879. This boy was an invalid from birth, so although he was eighteen when Lady Lytton sat next to the Duke at dinner, it would be natural for him to speak of "his little son." The boy died in 1902.

[4] Maid-of-Honour to the Queen. Yet another of Lady Lytton's cousins through the Ravensworths.

perfect manners. The boys were pages.[1] The Court was at half past three. I do enjoy seeing them so much. Lord Salisbury, with the Oxford deputation, spoke with great feeling and the words must have been put together by him for they were so beautiful. The Queen answered, "I thank you for this flattering, too flattering, address," in her most beautiful voice.

[The second volume of the diary ends here, but to the last page Lady Lytton had pinned these two newspaper cuttings:]

The following is a literal transcript of a letter received last week by her Majesty:

Address, The Queen, Windsor Castle:—
Dear Queen, — I want a pair of twins.
They must be a boy and a girl, and the
girl must be one minuit older than the
boy. Please send them quick — Your
affectionate subject, Blanche S — .
P.S. You sent me last Jubilee.

The Paris *Figaro* states that the Sèvres manufactory is busily engaged on porcelain busts of the Czar and Czarina in the execution of which their Majesties take great interest.[2]

[1] Lady Sophie Palmer was the unmarried sister of Lord Selborne who had married Lord Salisbury's elder daughter. Her nephews were Viscount Wolmer, born 1887, and Robert Palmer, born 1888. They were pages to Lord Salisbury on this occasion. Wang was their sister, Mabel, born 1884. She was always called Wang until in 1906 she married Earl Grey.

[2] The Tsar and Tsarina went over the Sèvres factory during their visit to France after their stay at Balmoral. They were on their way to Versailles and stopped there while their horses and escort were changed. The Tsar wrote to his mother that they had had "a close look over the famous factory and Museum," and that "a number of beautiful presents" were given to them.

Chapter Five

LADY LYTTON went again to Balmoral in October of this year, 1897. Lord Balfour of Burleigh was the Minister in Attendance when she arrived there. He was a representative peer and Secretary for Scotland with a seat in the Cabinet. On October 13 he was replaced as Minister in Attendance by Lord James of Hereford, Chancellor of the Duchy of Lancaster, who had been a brilliant barrister.

The Queen was very worried at this time about the fighting on the North-West Frontier which had broken out as a result of the widespread plague and famine in India. In all her communications with Lord Salisbury and Lord George Hamilton, Secretary of State for India, she stressed the admirable behaviour of the native princes and troops. In one cypher telegram to Lord George she wrote with great understanding: "I fear that the poor people are suffering from the necessity of supplying horses and ponies and cattle to us, as we have lost so many, which comes heavily upon them after their famine and plague. Would wish to know how many Native officers and men have been killed and wounded. The former are never mentioned, but only the English, which I think very wrong."

And in another telegram to Lord George on September 19 she hoped that the Victoria Cross would "be awarded equally to Native and British troops," and in one to Lord Salisbury on October 26 she was still harping on the matter: "The Victoria Cross should be bestowed equally on both [English and Native troops], and the distinction of race, so long and I think so unduly maintained, should disappear on such occasions. Lord George Hamilton only wants your and my support to carry this out."

Lady Lytton left home on her thirty-third wedding anniversary.

Balmoral. 5 October 1897

I had a cold journey from Hatfield to King's Cross and by ten a.m. Express to Aberdeen yesterday and felt sad on our wedding day, and thinking over servants' troubles at home, and all dear Vic's trials which make him low especially at home. Good night's rest at Aberdeen, at the Imperial Hotel, and walk about the town which is handsome but dreary and noisy and there was a high cold wind. Lunch at Ballater, Invercauld Arms, and drive over here with the carriage half open was nice though very cold. Harriet Phipps most kindly came to see me when free and I chatted with her in the drawing-room (which is left like last year for us and comfortable). Then I had a rest till half past five. Fanny Drummond who is always so nice to me is here. The Queen saw me in the passage as she came in, but the Royalties dined alone, as it was the anniversary of Prince Henry [of Battenberg]'s birthday.

October 6

Went out on a hired bicycle with Princess Beatrice. It was very nice but hot, the Princess chatted so pleasantly. Drove to Glenmuick to tea with Harriet, Fanny Drummond and Lord Balfour of Burleigh. Glenesks most cordial and full of their place at Cannes [the Château St Michel] just purchased for £20,000 all furnished and complete. Lord and Lady de l'Isle there. Nice walk home from Abergeldie with Lord B.B. who spoke of an excellent speech Robert [Lytton] had made at the Cecil Club,[1] said his work interested him much and that he always tried to appoint the best men to new posts no matter what was said. Evening rather stiff. Whist after the Queen left, which is so amusing.

October 7

Walked early before breakfast. To my surprise the Queen sent to me to be ready at 11.15 to walk by her chair as I had

---

[1] The Cecil Club was founded on 27 October 1882, when Lord Lytton, with many other prominent men of the day, was present. The object of the Club was to advance the interests of the Conservative Party in literary, artistic and scientific worlds. In 1949 the Cecil Club amalgamated with the United Club and has since been known as the United and Cecil Club.

not yet done this, but it was delightful and the Queen talked so much on all subjects. She hears Lord Elgin should have known the frontier troubles were coming and the Bombay plague may have influenced the Tribes.

At one, the Queen received deputations and addresses and I was present. The one of the Church of Scotland was so well worded and the Queen acknowledged it with her beautiful voice, "I thank you for this loyal address. I have always been devoted to Scotland and to the Church." Large lunch of thirty. Drove to Braemar and took Fanny Drummond to Lady Kennard.[1] Walked a mile and a half when near Balmoral, with such lovely moonlight. The Miss Eisslers played violin, harp and piano very well, the harp much the best.[2]

October 8

Showery but the air delicious. Went out before breakfast and before lunch and love the air. I drove with the Queen and Miss Majendie and had a good tea at one of the lodges in the Forest. Aline and I had a walk after in the moonlight. Lord Rowton, Mr Chaplin [President of the Local Government Board, afterwards Viscount Chaplin] and two Miss Farquharsons [daughters of Lieut-Colonel Ross Farquharson of Invercauld] to dinner.

October 9

Nice walk and talk with Lord Rowton to Mrs Symon's shop, and to get honey from the Bootmaker, 1/1 a lb. Back through the wood.

[Mrs Symon died the following January. The Queen, at Osborne, wrote in her journal on January 27: "Heard when we were at breakfast from Mr Forbes [the factor] that dear old Mrs Symon at the shop in the village at Balmoral had

---

[1] Lady Kennard had in 1891 been raised to the rank of Baronet's widow as the Queen had signified her intention of bestowing a Baronetcy upon her husband, Coleridge Kennard, M.P. for Salisbury, who died in 1890. Her grandson received the title.

[2] The Misses Eissler are mentioned in unpublished parts of Queen Victoria's journal, but no details are given beyond the fact that they were three sisters. They performed several times before the Queen.

passed away. Though she had recovered so well while we were there and greeted us as kindly as ever, she caught a chill a few days ago and was carried off by bronchitis. We had found her and her good amusing husband in the village when we first came to Balmoral in 1848, and we built them their new house and shop. She was quite an institution; and everyone, high and low, used to go and see her." The morning after the Tsarina arrived at Balmoral in September 1896, she took the Tsar to see Mrs Symon and they bought up most of the shop, which sold a little of everything from gingerbread to fishing rods.]

October 10

Service in the Chapel. Dr Cameron Lees [Dean of the Chapels Royal for Scotland and Minister of St Giles's Edinburgh] very good prayers and sermon. Nice walk though windy to Flag Staff before luncheon. Afternoon walked up the hill behind the Church with Lord Balfour who walks and talks very cheerily. The wind knocked me down about three times but I laughed and enjoyed it. Lord B. of B. told me of his getting into the House of Lords by election at twenty-eight, and he prepared different speeches fifteen times and then spoke without preparation but on a subject he knew well, so he could be useful and it gave him a good start. The Dee in flood looked splendid. Cheery evening with letter game, and Princess Beatrice merrier than she has yet been since her sorrow.

October 11

Short walk before breakfast and to see Mr Donald Stewart [the head keeper]. Lady Kennard and Fanny Drummond called and Miss F. Wilson, a funny type. She gives £500 for four months at Invercauld for the old Tower and near proximity of Balmoral.

[Miss Fleetwood-Wilson had rented Old Mar Castle (Braemar Castle) from the Farquharsons of Invercauld. She was a very rich woman who lived at 30 Portman Square. She was most kind and hospitable but something of an invalid. A young friend who stayed with her that autumn said that she "had to be kept together in iron stays." The following summer she married Prince Alexis Dolgorouki, the youngest son of Prince Dolgorouki who was Secretary of State and Privy Seal to the Tsar. After her marriage she had no more need for the "near proximity of Balmoral" as the Prince, who was said to have married her to pay his gambling debts, considered himself more royal than anyone there. Nevertheless they continued for some years to go to Braemar Castle every autumn, and lavishly entertained there. The Princess was famous for her jewels. In 1908 Edwin Lutyens built a house for her, Nashdown, at Taplow, estimated at £15,000.]

October 12

Nice walks before breakfast and lunch. Little drive in snow showers and bitter cold round the Hill with Harriet, and to tea with Lady Edwards. I walked home and the air was so pure though cold. A gentleman to sing in the evening, good voice and enunciation, but not a true artist and an American. I sat by the Queen and brought up the singer twice but, Oh, it was such a stiff circle.

October 13

Very cold and frosty. Drove with the Queen and Harriet. The Queen said the Council had been short and [they] always were as no discussion takes place or anything of interest and had not since George IV's time. Pleasant tea, Lord James, Fritz Ponsonby and Lord William Cecil [Groom-in-Waiting]. Quiet evening, rooms so cold for low dresses.

October 14

Lovely day, air like crystal, atmosphere so clear and every little chimney smoke going up looked effective. Clouds and colouring lovely.

Went on the hill before breakfast. Eight degrees of frost had bowed the sweet peas and flowers.

Before lunch went up the Corndavon Road and thought of the past and my dear Neville travelling back to Paris,

God Bless him. I notice all so keenly when alone and the burn and dashing Dee are so full of life.

Drove with Harriet and Bessy Bulteel by the wild heather, the road that comes out by Invercauld.

Henry Whites dined, she looking so pretty and her gentle voice seemed to please the Queen.[1]

October 16

Lord James in great spirits after a day with gout in his room and he is a brilliant talker. He taught me a patience before tea and Bridge-Whist at eleven.

[The game of Bridge is said to have been invented in Eastern Europe, possibly in Greece, and was very popular in Constantinople and Athens in the eighties. It was first known by the name of Biritch or Russian Whist, which gave rise to the erroneous idea that it was of Russian origin. This name was contracted into Bridge. In the autumn of 1894 it was introduced into the Portland Club by Lord Brougham who had learnt to play it on a recent visit to Cairo. It differed from Whist in that the dealer could either nominate trumps or leave it to his partner to do so. In the spring of 1899 the *Lady's Realm* reported that "All the papers have been full of a game which has been made fashionable by Society, and which is called Bridge. It has certainly been a great rage and was a source of amusement to a great many during the long winter evenings between five and seven. It is a species of whist which is played by four people, but one hand is laid on the table for everyone to see, so it can quite easily be played by three and it is certainly a better game than Dummy Whist. The game is called Bridge because, owing to certain rules and complications which occur in the game, it is possible to 'bridge' or pass over when it is your turn to play. It is a great gambling game, and a great deal may be won or lost in one night, as the bets can be doubled at will, and the points are generally high."

[1] Henry White was First Secretary at the American Embassy in London. (The American Legation was raised to the status of Embassy in 1893.) He had married in 1879 Margaret Stuyvesant Rutherfurd. They were staying at Braemar.

Auction Bridge originated in India in 1903 and was a game for only three players until the Bath Club turned it, in 1906, into a four-handed game. Although Whist is still a very popular game, Bridge in its early form, as taught to Lady Lytton by Lord James and described by the *Lady's Realm*, is never played now.]

October 17

Drove to call on Miss Wilson with Bessy Bulteel, Lord James and Lord W. Cecil. That old Mar Castle is so wonderfully done up and looks very nice. We received a strange (to us) guest, a Captain Forbes, then a Mrs Graham came in and Mr Edwards, and when tea had been brought in the hostess herself arrived and she is like a little sprite. Nice drive back and not cold.

Sunday, October 18

In Chapel we had Sullivan's Jubilee Hymn, and it was nice singing it behind the Queen. Mr Williamson gave a good Sermon.[1] The Queen walked up and down the steps. There was a great gale all day but as I was going out at a quarter to five I heard I was to drive with the Queen, and was alone with her. She asked if it would hurt the horses or coachman but never thought of herself. I spoke of Con being so good to me and she said, "Oh you must not say that, children ought never to think they can do enough for their parents." And she said she never read a novel till she married, and had been very careful what books her daughters read, and she thought even Scott was sometimes coarse. It was very nice talking with her Majesty alone. Pleasant dinner between Lord James and Sir Fleetwood Edwards.

October 19

Still a gale but warm and bright and I again enjoyed my walks and thoughts for the future. The Queen gave me her

[1] Dr Wallace Williamson was Minister of St Cuthbert's Parish Church, Edinburgh, and afterwards of St Giles's Cathedral, Edinburgh.

Jubilee photo and a water colour sketch by Mr Otherwell of Invercauld which is pretty.[1]

Picked leaves and berries to leave for Emily Ampthill. In the afternoon Aline [Majendie] and I drove behind the Queen and Princess Hohenlohe[2] to the Falls of Garrawald [Garbh Allt] and they were full and lovely with just an orange red mountain ash tree in the foreground and we walked up at the end and then drove to the Forest Lodge for tea, where the Queen and Princess were very cheerful. We talked of people having a lot of dresses for change, and the Queen who is so simple said it was very unnecessary, as long as one had appropriate dresses. The Queen had a good appetite and after two scones, two bits of toast and several biscuits she said, "I am afraid I must not have any more."

Musical Artists in the evening, but the pieces badly selected and Albani's voice is not what it used to be, and Fanny Davies is not really good at the piano. I had difficulty in placing the ladies and presenting some ladies to Princess Hohenlohe but I was never warned so had to do as best I could. The Queen took leave of me in the corridor after the Concert was over. Not in bed till half past one and woke at six.

October 20

Glorious fine morning like summer. Left Balmoral at half past nine. Aline and Bessy Bulteel came to say good-bye. Lovely drive to Ballater and the hills so clear. Met Alick Yorke going into waiting. Saw Emily Ampthill at Aberdeen with headache. Dear Bets [her daughter Betty Balfour] met me at Edinburgh and it was so nice and we talked much going to Whittingehame [Arthur Balfour's house in East Lothian] where I spent a happy day and two nights and then home to the Danes.

[At the beginning of the next year, 1898, there were many political anxieties. Fighting was still going on on the North-

[1] She must have meant B. J. Ottewell, a painter in water colour, who exhibited at the Royal Academy.
[2] Alexandra (Sandra), third daughter of the Duke of Edinburgh (Coburg), who had married in April 1896, Ernest, Hereditary Prince of Hohenlohe-Langenburg, the Queen's great-nephew through her half-sister, Feodora. Prince and Princess Ernest were both staying at Balmoral.

West Frontier which troubled the Queen greatly; the Sultan
was making difficulties over Crete; but more important than
anything Sir Herbert Kitchener had at last begun in earnest the
long-planned campaign for the reconquest of the Sudan "for
civilisation," which had been held up for almost two years
while careful preparations were going on. In January
British troops in Egypt were sent up the Nile, and Kitchener
asked for reinforcements from England. By the first week in
September the whole of the Sudan had been recovered. This
victorious campaign, however, almost led to war with France,
for when Kitchener reached Khartoum, where he went
immediately after the fall of Omdurman on September 2nd,
he heard that Major Marchand, with a detachment, was in
possession of Fashoda, a village on the White Nile, three
hundred miles south of Khartoum, where he had hoisted the
French flag. The British would not tolerate any civilising
influence in the Sudan other than their own, and Kitchener
hurried to Fashoda to hoist the Egyptian flag beside the
tricolour (*not* the British flag for fear of precipitating trouble).
Marchand refused to withdraw without orders from his
government and the situation was tense for several months,
until eventually the French Government gave in and
Marchand was recalled. France did not easily forgive the
"insult of Fashoda," and for a long time bore bitter resent-
ment against England. But when Lady Lytton went into
waiting at Osborne in February the campaign was still in its
infancy.]

Osborne. 8 *February* 1898

Came to Osborne. Lovely day for the journey but the
boat rocked rather. Maggie Ponsonby and Mrs Eliot
Yorke[1] came over with me and I went with Annie [Yorke]
in her carriage. I did not see the Queen till dinner time, but
was so glad that H.M. looked quite wonderfully well and
younger than she had done for the last two years. She spoke

[1] Widow of the Hon. Eliot Yorke, Lady Lytton's first cousin, who had been
an Equerry to the Duke of Edinburgh. She was a daughter of Lord Rothschild
and lived at Hamble Cliff, Netley, Portsmouth. Her father-in-law, Lord
Hardwicke, had a house on the Isle of Wight. Maggie Ponsonby was Sir
Henry Ponsonby's younger daughter who never married.

to me in the evening with great feeling of dear Alice Lathom's great loss and thought it seemed so unnecessary.[1] Princess Louis of Battenberg and Princess Beatrice are the only Princesses here. I was glad to find Harriet Phipps still here and she came to my room after tea for a little talk. She said the Queen did not wish us to talk politics as the times were too anxious. Aline Majendie and Mary Hughes are the two nice maids-of-honour and Mrs Grant has come already to relieve Harriet.

February 9

I showed Annie Yorke the Indian and other rooms with Lord Edward Clinton and they looked lovely with bright sunshine.[2] I drove with the Queen and Princess Beatrice in the afternoon.

February 10

Fine after rain and lovely sun at midday. I drove again with the Queen and Aline Majendie. The Queen spoke of its being her fifty-eighth wedding day and named all her bridesmaids to us, and said Sir Henry Byng had been a page at that ceremony, and here he was as Equerry to-day, and wrote to the Queen this morning.[3]

In the evening there was such a good Marine band from Portsmouth beginning at dinner with the Wedding March which pleased the Queen and she enjoyed it and looked so well. Lord Cross [Lord Privy Seal] was there. In the evening Sir Henry Byng said he remembered the wedding so well and a dinner and Ball at Stafford House after.

February 11

Very pleasant day to Netley[4] with the Queen, Princess

[1] On November 23 Lady Lathom, wife of the Lord Chamberlain and Lady Lytton's first cousin, was driving her pony-carriage in Lathom Park, Ormskirk, Lancashire, when the pony either shied or bolted, the carriage fell into the lake and she was drowned.

[2] The Indian Room, or Durbar Room, was completed in 1892.

[3] Sir Henry Byng was staying at Osborne but he wrote to the Queen as was the Household practice. In 1898 he succeeded his brother as 4th Earl of Strafford, and died in 1899.

[4] The Royal Victoria Hospital, Netley, was a Military Hospital and Army Medical School just outside Portsmouth. The Queen had laid the foundation

Beatrice and Princess Louis of Battenberg. Lovely weather and reception most cordial. There were not many wounded from India, but some who were mere boys. I thought the Queen might be tired with all the changes but she said, Oh, no it was all so easily managed, and she drove after her lunch for half an hour at five. Her health and strength are wonderful, thank God. A nice ladies' dinner.

February 12

Dear Con's birthday and how many good things I wished for her. I told Aline and she came out with me. Harriet Phipps left after lunch, but I have not been able to see her much she has been so busy writing and winding up business. Drove with Mary Hughes to Parkhurst [the Island Garrison] and had not been there since I was twelve! The Cowes Amateur Spring Band played so well in the evening.

February 13

Very dull Sunday Service in the Chapel and no going out with rain before luncheon. I went to the Swiss Cottage with Fräulein Bauer[1] where all the Princes and Princesses have collected quite interesting things.

[The Swiss Cottage, half a mile east of Osborne House, along an avenue called High Walk, was brought in sections from Switzerland and erected in 1853–54 under the supervision of Prince Albert. Here the Royal children learnt to cook their own garden produce on small-scale stoves, and serve it to their parents as a special treat. All the children had patches of flower and vegetable gardens of their own, and their own tools and wheelbarrows with their initials on them were kept in an adjoining shed. Close by was another building which housed the museum full of treasures collected by the children themselves, mostly specimens of natural history. The Swiss Cottage and museum, and the children's

stone in May 1856. The main hospital was closed in 1956, and the present hospital is now used almost entirely for the treatment of psychiatric cases in the Army.

[1] Princess Beatrice's former German Governess, officially described as *Lectrice* to the Queen's Household.

garden tools, can be seen to-day quite untouched, and also the Queen's bathing machine which has now been placed there, complete with the iron track on which it ran down into the sea.]

I felt very low-spirited as the climate is depressing and I feel I have so little vitality to help the life, and long meals. Ladies' dinner with only Mrs Grant, myself, Lady and Miss Cowell, who hardly spoke. Princess Beatrice talked all dinner time easily, but the Queen spoke but little then, or in the evening, and as Princess Beatrice left early it was very solemn and made me so nervous.[1]

February 14

Aline and I had to go to a School Entertainment at Whippingham with acting, songs, recitations etc. Rather hot and trying for two hours, but they are well trained. Lady Emma Crichton arrived to tea. Lord Northbrook, Colonel Crichton, Lord A. Russell, Lieut.-General Nash at dinner in the Indian Room.[2] Lord Northbrook was very cheerful and chatty. General Nash told me the Queen was giving extra good wooden legs to the men who had lost them, besides armchairs for Netley.

February 15

Most lovely clear day and sun but a very high wind and everyone wondering if we should leave Osborne as arranged. Fräulein Bauer told us after breakfast Princess Beatrice had been seized with violent sciatica and could not move or dress, but then there were fresh speculations but soon the decision came that the Queen would go and Princess Beatrice

[1] Princess Beatrice had her own wing at Osborne.

[2] Surgeon-Major-General William Nash had recently been appointed Principal Medical Officer of the Royal Victoria Hospital, Netley. He had been Principal Medical Officer of the Army of Occupation in Egypt for the past three years. Lady Emma Crichton was the daughter of Lord Northbrook who had preceded Lord Lytton as Governor-General of India. She had married in 1890 Colonel Crichton, Hon. Colonel of the Hampshire Imperial Yeomanry and a brother of the 4th Earl of Erne. Lord Alexander Russell, son of the 6th Duke of Bedford, was Colonel-Commandant of the Rifle Brigade. Lord Northbrook was Lord-Lieutenant of Hampshire.

remain at Osborne with Fräulein Bauer who was in such a state because even "de slippers and de nightgown" had gone on to Windsor. I like her so much. We left after luncheon and had quite a good crossing with favourable wind and tide, but I never saw the Solent with such waves.

The Special new train glided so comfortably from Portsmouth to Windsor. The new station there is quite imposing.[1] Ladies' dinner, and I sat by the Queen but the talk was so easy, *and* in the evening.

February 17

Very cold but dry. Walk with Aline in the morning. Drove to Cumberland Lodge, bitter wind. Sat by the Queen again at dinner, she seemed so well and inclined to talk till eleven. Lady Biddulph and the Dean [of Windsor] and Mrs Eliot dined.

February 18

Horrid cold snowy day. Did not go out. Mr Donaldson called though I had told him not because of the measles at Eton. He looked so well and stout and hopes to quite recover his illness, and asked much after Vic and Nev. Sydney Earle[2] came to tea and was so easy and nice with the ladies and after alone with me.

Prince and Princess Christian and Prince Christle [Prince Christian Victor, their elder son] dined, and Lord Lorne and Lord Salisbury who talked most cheerily. The evening was rather dull.

February 19

Bitter cold day that made one's face ache. Drove with the Queen and Princess Louis of B. I was sheltered sitting back. The wind hurt the Queen's eyes so she shut them and it made her sleepy coming back, but she struggled against it so well

---

[1] Most of the railway companies either improved existing trains or designed new ones during the Diamond Jubilee year, when the new station at Windsor was opened.

[2] The eldest son of Mrs Charles Earle, Lady Lytton's sister. He was killed in the Boer War.

9

as the Princess helped by questions. Dinner of twelve.
Duke and Duchess of Connaught and the Duke and Duchess
of York, the latter looking ill and so sad, but speaking very
nicely of her mother's death and sorrow.[1]

February 20

Sunday and good sermon from the Dean of Worcester
[R. W. Forrest] on the importance of personal influence and
character. He mentioned one poor woman who always sent to
him to beg him to thank God on her behalf the day when she
first became bedridden, and that it has a marvellous effect on
so many people, and it made one remember how wonderful
is the example of the Queen's wonderful strength and personal character. Beloved Con came at three all the way from
Surrey to London to see Adela [Villiers, Lady Lytton's
niece] and the Ponsonbys and down here to me, and was so
brilliant and beloved. I saw her off at six with Maggie
Ponsonby wondering how she would manage to get back by
night, but all went well she wired the next morning. Blessings
on her for coming. Princess Beatrice dined again and it was
nice to see her.

February 21

Twelve degrees of frost and fog early but lovely later.
Walked with A. Majendie to Frogmore; the sight of the green-
house was enchanting, but walk back tiring. After lunch
Fräulein Bauer showed me some rooms I had not seen before.
The Ewarts and Kennedys[2] to dinner and it went off well.

[Lady Lytton left Windsor the following morning and the
next entry in her diary takes up only half a page:]

Went to Osborne August 9 and had such glorious summer
weather and we sat out under the tree all day. The Duke and
Duchess of York and dear children were there and Princess

---

[1] The Duchess of Teck had died of heart failure after a sudden operation on
27 October 1897. She was a well-known and beloved figure in England.

[2] Mr Gordon Kennedy had just been appointed Minister at Bucharest. He was
knighted in 1901.

Aribert[1] who is so pretty and Princess Victoria of S. Holstein [Thora] and the Duke and Duchess of Connaught and family. And the Queen gave me a photo later at Balmoral.

I went twice on board the Prince of Wales's yacht [the *Osborne*] with the Queen, and the first time went to speak to him; and he was so patient after his accident and looked so happy and said he had no pain.[2]

[In October, when Lady Lytton again went to Balmoral, the Empress Frederick was staying there. This was the first time for fourteen years that the Empress had been to the Castle and the first time since her husband's death. She had become engaged at Balmoral, so it held bitter-sweet memories for her. She had arrived in England at the end of September and was to stay until after Christmas. Her second daughter, Victoria, was with her at Balmoral. This girl, who was now twenty-four, had been prevented by Bismarck from marrying the man she loved, Alexander of Battenberg, Prince of Bulgaria. A secret engagement between them, kept going largely by the Empress who was determined that her daughter's happiness should not be ruined, had dragged on for some years, until 1889, when Alexander, after his abdication, finally extricated himself and married an actress. A year later Victoria married Prince Adolf of Schaumburg-Lippe, but she was not happy, for the years went by and she had no children. Prince Adolf died in 1916, and thirteen years later she married a Russian adventurer, Alexander Zoubkoff, young enough to be her grandson, who left her after a year, taking her money with him. She died soon afterwards at Bonn as the result of a chill caught during a despairing walk along the river bank.

This was to prove the Empress's last visit to England. On September 4 she had had a fall from her horse at her home

[1] Princess Aribert of Anhalt, better known as Princess Marie Louise, was the younger daughter of Prince and Princess Christian. She was now separated from Prince Aribert whom she had married in 1891. The marriage was annulled in 1900.

[2] In July, while visiting Waddesdon, Ferdinand de Rothschild's house, the Prince of Wales had fallen down a spiral staircase and fractured his knee-cap. Ferdinand de Rothschild, who was one of his greatest friends, died in December of that year, 1898.

at Friedrichshof near Hamburg which precipitated the cancer of the spine from which she died. Her first symptoms of pain were put down to lumbago, and even after she herself had discovered what was wrong with her, she gave out to the world that it was lumbago from which she was suffering. She died after fearful pain on 5 August 1901, at the age of sixty, six months after her mother.

There was only one long entry in Lady Lytton's diary that autumn.]

Balmoral Castle, 11 *October* 1898

I have been here a week, arriving on the 4th of October, our wedding day, in lovely summer weather. The Empress Frederick is here and her daughter, Princess Victoria of Schaumburg-Lippe and Prince Adolf. The second morning the Empress called on me, and I went with her, Countess Perponcher and Count Seckendorff for a walk to see the Church which she much admired, and the memorial window [to her father] which she chose was carried out by Clayton and Bell.[1]

I drove with the Queen Friday, Sunday and Monday, and she was not tired or sleepy and so very nice and kind.

Mary Hughes was at her best and I felt quite sorry when she left on Monday, the 10th, and Fanny Lambart came and was so sad at her mother's illness and death.

Lord Balfour of Burleigh came Friday to Tuesday. I had a nice walk with him from Abergeldie Mains[2] on Saturday and he told me about not going to India, and he is very pleased at the birth of a baby daughter after fifteen years' interval, and the Queen says she will be godmother and send a little locket.[3]

[1] Clayton and Bell, Stained Glass Artists, 311 Regent Street, received the Royal Warrant in 1898. All too soon the Empress's own monument was to go up on the east wall of the Church: "To Victoria Adelaide Mary Louise, German Empress and Queen of Prussia, Princess Royal of Great Britain and Ireland."

[2] A house belonging to the Abergeldie Castle estate, leased by the Crown. Visitors were often put up there.

[3] Lord Balfour already had two daughters and two sons, the youngest, George, born in 1883. The new baby was christened Victoria Alexandrina Catherine. She had a distinguished career in the prison service, being the first

To-day, October 11th, began by being damp and frosty, then it rained a little and after got fine. I walked half an hour before breakfast, then to the Corndavon Road with Countess Perponcher who is very pleasant to talk with. And in the afternoon I walked alone with the Empress Frederick and she talks so easily and pleasantly, and went up the Forest to the Cairn put up on the 11th October, 1852, to commemorate the purchase of Balmoral,[1] then went to tea at the Donald Stewarts'.

I was walking away but was sent for to join Princess Beatrice and the Prince of Wales[2] and it was so nice and interesting. The French actresses were discussed and talk very cheery. The Prince fears there will be difficulties to hold the exhibition of 1900 at Paris. I wonder how it will be.

[In January of the previous year, 1897, the Prince of Wales, in order to foster better relations between England and France, which had been strained by the tension over Fashoda, had agreed to become President of the British Commission of the International Exhibition to be held in Paris in 1900. He immensely enjoyed his role, and in 1899 went over to Paris to watch the Exhibition buildings going up, but by the end of that year there was so much anti-British feeling in the French press over the South African war, and so much sympathy shown for the Boers, that the Prince told Lord Salisbury that he wished to withdraw from the Presidency. He was persuaded, however, to stay on as his withdrawal would only increase France's bad feeling against England, but before the opening of the Exhibition on April 15, personal abuse of the Queen had become so virulent that he refused to attend the inaugural ceremony for fear that the Paris mob might insult the British uniform he would be

woman to be appointed Governor of the Duke Street Prison in Glasgow. Lord Balfour had been sounded on going to India as Viceroy. One of the reasons, probably the main one, which compelled him to refuse was the age of his mother which precluded an absence for so long as five years.

[1] The Queen's own description of the building of this Cairn is given in Appendix G on p. 166.

[2] The Prince of Wales was staying with his eldest daughter, the Duchess of Fife, at New Mar Lodge. The Fifes had just moved into the new house.

wearing, and lest his presence might be taken for indifference
to the insults to the Queen. The Queen was in agreement
with him and put off her own holiday to Cimiez. Nor would
she go to Italy, for it would mean passing through France.
Instead she went to Ireland.]

Dear Ernest [her brother] and Lord Acton [Lord-in-
Waiting] dined which was so nice.

Glenesk says Dreyfus had risen from his ability in the
French army to a very good position and was requested by
the Headquarters staff to write a report to the Army to send
to Russia but when the report was read by the *Corps d'Armée*
they missed some details giving more artillery and Infantry
than really existed and which Dreyfus explained were not
really there. This made a bad feeling against him and so he
was much watched, and like other Jews he was curious and
asked many questions about Forts and guns and things all
round, when the word was started of espionage and so the
feeling grew, and every suspicion was exaggerated and papers
drawn up of accusation till all believed he was really guilty,
but they went through dishonourable ways to prove it—
and the whole *Corps d'Armée* now seems to blame.

The Queen took me alone with her when she went to visit
Glenesk, and she took a little tea and had a quiet talk with
him for about twenty minutes. Glenesk looks so very sad at
his great loss.[1]

[Although Dreyfus had been found guilty and degraded in
January 1895, and sent to the Devil's Island a month later, it
was not until three years afterwards, with the publication in
Aurore, on 13 January 1898, of Zola's famous open letter,
J'Accuse, that the public outside France began to take an
interest in his fate. On September 4 Mme Dreyfus had
filed an appeal to the Minister of Justice who laid the case
before the Court of Appeal. So far, few of the true facts had
come to light, so it is not surprising that Lord Glenesk's
account of how Dreyfus came to be accused and tried should

[1] Lady Glenesk had died suddenly of heart failure that summer at their villa
at Cannes at the age of fifty-five.

have been so vague, especially when muddled by Lady Lytton, but he was right in saying that Dreyfus's accusers really believed him to be guilty. From now on the case was to be more and more discussed until people could talk of little else. In England public opinion was almost entirely on the side of Dreyfus, whereas in France it remained divided.]

Chapter Six

THE Empress Frederick was still in England when Lady Lytton went to Osborne in the following January. The Empress had spent Christmas with her mother at Osborne. The Queen invariably went to Osborne for Christmas. The Empress had intended to leave England for Bordighera at the beginning of January but Count Seckendorff was ill and could not be moved until the 12th. She found it very provoking, for although she was not sorry to be kept a few more days in England, her rooms at the Hotel Augst in Bordighera had been taken and were being paid for.

This was the last year that Lady Lytton kept a diary.

Osborne. 14 January 1899

I came here on the 10th and brought Neville's portraits of Ruth, baby Barbara and Eddie Marsh.[1] The Empress Frederick sent for me at seven to see them, and gave them a few minutes attention though busy writing. She was puzzled by so much colour being mixed together and said it was the present French school. She liked the study of Eddie the best, and drawing of the ear. In the evening the Queen told me to send them to her, which I did the next day, and she praised them very much, and liked the baby and she sent for them the next day to show to the Princess [Beatrice]. The Empress Frederick left the next morning. Count Seckendorff has been laid up with heart weakness for some weeks but was able to start under the care of Dr Woods whom the Queen sends to Berlin.

Sir James Reid I hear thinks badly of the case but the

---

[1] A great friend of Neville's, afterwards Sir Edward Marsh. Ruth was Betty Balfour's eldest little girl, aged nine. Baby Barbara was Emily Lutyens's first baby, born 8 August 1898. G. F. Watts's opinion of two of these pictures is given in Appendix H on p. 167.

Empress differs from him, and Sir Charles Laking thought at first it was not so bad, and then that it was.[1] I hope he may get to Berlin.

Admiral Fullerton told me he was trying to arrange for the Queen to go abroad by Folkestone and Boulogne, which would be a shorter passage, and she did not like a wave breaking into her cabin last year with the ports open.

[The Queen had written in her Journal on 11 March 1898: *"Victoria and Albert*, Cherbourg—Arrived here at 4.30 after a rough disagreeable crossing, which tried me a good deal, though I was not sick. We had been told that the sea would be perfectly smooth, but it began rolling soon after I went below, and in the middle of the Channel there was one lurch just as if the ship had had a blow, the port hole burst half open, the sea came in and the chairs were sent spinning. The maids, steward and footmen all rushed in, in a great state, and found part of the cabin full of water. I was taken in the rolling chair across to my bedroom, where I got on to the sofa feeling much upset. Was very thankful when we got to Cherbourg at last. We had been misinformed about the weather."]

Heard of dear Edith Wilbraham's death on the 12th at 2 a.m., a mercy for her, after great suffering, but, Oh, how cruel for the dear sisters, and Reggie returning from the Cape on the 14th.[2]

Princess Christian and Thora with Countess E [Baroness Egloffstein, Lady-in-Waiting] arrived the 13th and were very cheery.

Prince and Princess Louis of Battenberg are also here.

[1] She meant Sir Francis Laking, Surgeon Apothecary to the Queen's Household and to that of the Prince of Wales. The Empress complained in a letter to Sophie on January 13: "Poor Conte is still very weak . . . it will be months before he is fit for work again."

[2] Edith Wilbraham was the youngest of Lord Lathom's five daughters. This was a tragic family. Lady Lathom had been drowned the year before, and Lord Lathom himself was to die in November. His eldest son, who succeeded him, died in 1910, and Reginald, the youngest of three brothers died in 1912. His second son also died young, and the title became extinct in 1930 on the death of his only grandson.

He is so like Prince Henry and she very clever and cheery talker. We have had three days of awful rain and gales. Lovely the 14th, like Italy.

Monday, 16th and Wednesday, 18th there were very nice concerts in the Durbar Room. Clara Butt sang well and is much improved at the first concert, and Mr Rumford and Herr Wolff (violin) at the second. It was nice to see the Queen at a party and she enjoyed it and was so keen and it was quite a treat for us all and the stand-up supper after was so nice as one could move about.[1]

The Band [of the Royal Marine Light Infantry] also played the 17th in the evening. The 17th there was a large luncheon for the President of Costa Rica [Señor Rafael Iglesias], a strong intelligent looking man. He was much distressed, he told Princess Christian, that people asked him in London if his people were savages and wore no clothes! He told Mr Synge [Clerk in the Treaty Department of the Foreign Office] after he was delighted with his reception and the Queen's kindness. In the evening I had a pleasant walk with Colonel Clerk to see Princess Beatrice's Osborne Cottages, then round by Norris and over some palings and back by the park,[2] so I did not go out till tea-time when Aline and I went to their [the Battenberg children's] tea party, which was very cheery, with games and charade and a little dancing. The Battenberg children came to tea with us on the 19th and were such natural dear ones, the two eldest, Drino and Ena much quieter and controlled, but Leopold and Maurice very scampish, and yet one dreads Prince Leopold hurting himself.[3] The Queen driving the 19th when I was

[1] Kennerley Rumford, baritone, married Clara Butt in 1900. In the diary was enclosed a note which Miss Phipps sent to Lady Lytton on the 16th saying: "The Queen advises you to bring a smelling bottle with you to-night in case the room gets too hot."

[2] Norris Castle and its beautiful park adjoin Osborne and were part of the Osborne estate. Victoria had stayed there as a child with her mother. It had been designed by Wyatt for Lord Henry Seymour. Albert Cottages were being built for Princess Beatrice's children when they were at Osborne, though they were still to live with the Queen at Windsor and Balmoral.

[3] Prince Leopold suffered from haemophilia. He was always delicate and a great anxiety, but he lived until 1922. Ena was Princess Victoria Eugénie, born 1887, Princess Beatrice's only daughter. In 1906 she married King Alfonso of Spain.

with her was quite nervous because of the great gale and the four horses, but all went quietly.

January 20

The memorial service for Prince Henry of Battenberg was very touching and nice, but it is a mistake so many going to it now it is a third year. Princess B is very brave, and her lady, Miss Minnie Cochrane, and Colonel Clerk are devoted to her.

The Bishop of Winchester [Randall Davidson] came from Saturday to Monday and I had two very pleasant dinners by him, and his sermon on Sunday 23rd was admirable and it is a real privilege to hear him. The difficulties of the present day are very great in the Church and Mr Harcourt is an old-fashioned Whig and cannot help really, but the Bishop of W. had been corresponding with him and is going to see him.[1]

My last night, 23rd January, Arthur Balfour was there and so pleasant, praising the dear children's play [Betty Balfour's children] and Betty's work. "She is too diffident," he added. "Do you think Colley's life will interfere with Betty's?" [Lady Lytton asked]. "Oh, no, not at all." Then speaking of Colley's reverses, "Military matters in any country cannot always succeed, but the shame was never avenging Majuba."

[General Sir George Colley, who, as has already been said, was Private Secretary to Lord Lytton when he was Viceroy of India, had been killed on 26 February 1881 at Majuba Hill, a bitter defeat when the Boers routed six hundred British troops under Colley's command. W. F. Butler had just written a life of Colley and Lady Lytton was afraid that it might conflict with Betty Balfour's book on her father, *The History of Lord Lytton's Administration 1876–1880*. Both books were published that year.

On May 24 the Queen celebrated her eightieth birthday

[1] She must have meant Sir William Harcourt, leader of the Liberal Party until 1898, whose violent letters attacking ritualism in the Church of England were then appearing in *The Times*. It is odd, though, that she did not know, or had forgotten, that he was knighted, seeing that his first wife, Thérèse Lister, who died in 1863, was her own first cousin (the elder sister of Lady Glenesk); but as he was not knighted until 1873, perhaps she still thought of him as he had been when he was her cousin by marriage.

at Windsor. She received presents from all her family, Household and friends, and many more letters and telegrams than at the Jubilee. All her children joined in giving her "three very handsome silver candelabras for the Durbar-room at Osborne," while the old Duke of Cambridge gave her "a beautiful miniature of George III set in diamonds, which had belonged to one of his aunts." In the evening the first, third and last acts of *Lohengrin*, with Jean and Edouard de Reszke as Lohengrin and Heinrich der Vogler, were given in the Waterloo Gallery, and the Queen declared herself "simply enchanted. It is the most glorious composition, so poetic, so dramatic, and one might almost say, religious in feeling and full of sadness, pathos and tenderness. The singing of the two brothers was beyond praise. . . . The whole opera produced a great impression on me."

Lady Lytton was not in waiting for the birthday but she joined the party at Windsor for dinner on the 26th and travelled up with the Queen to Balmoral that night. She kept no diary during this visit but there are two draft letters to her daughter, Constance, copied into her diary.]

Balmoral Castle   27 *May* 1899

Beloved Con,

The dinner was very pleasant in the big dining-room at Windsor, and Aline [Majendie] and Marie [Mallet] kept on their bonnets so my travelling attire was quite all right. Lord Edward Clinton took me in and no one came the other side, but the mild German Müther[1] was within talking distance.

Marie, Aline and I with the Baroness de Grancy who is in waiting on the Grand Duchess of Hesse [the Tsarina's sister-in-law, Ducky] are the ladies, and Sir Fleetwood Edwards, Sir John M'Neil, and Colonel Davidson the gentlemen besides Sir James Reid and Herr Müther. Marie looked very black and solemn and Aline told me this morning she could not

---

[1] Maurice Müther, the German Secretary. He was in charge of the archives at Windsor.

recover the blow of having to replace Harriet here now [until June 8 when Miss Phipps arrived].

I heard but few details about the birthday functions except that all had gone off without a hitch and the opera had been very good. The Queen received more telegrams than even at the Jubilee time—two thousand I heard first, and at dinner to-night the Queen said nearly four thousand. But I will inquire if the precise number is known. Imagine the trouble for clerks and secretaries. The singing in the Courtyard had been disappointing Lord Edward thought. We left the Castle at 8.15 and were shown to our carriages before the Queen and then we silently steamed away. Our carriages were very nice, but to be alone I took rather a cold end sleeping place—but all the carriages were *heated* which made such a difference. The sitting-room had a nice round table so I played Patience, not to go to bed too early, and some coffee and tea were offered at eleven, and I only took hot water. I read till past twelve in my compartment and then dozed very comfortably but always hearing the noise of the train though I slept sounder in the morning.

The sun rose so clear, and all day the weather had been lovely and much warmer than the last days at the Danes or Windsor, though they have been having ten degrees of frost even last night here. We had luxurious breakfast at Perth with beautiful hot-house fruit sent in of all kinds. We lunched in the train between Aberdeen and Ballater.

The drive from Ballater, Marie and I with Princess Ena, was lovely and not a bit cold, and we were just behind the Queen. The Queen's tenants and servants met her in Highland dress at the gates and presented an address and then walked each side of her carriage to the Castle playing on the bag-pipes. I was so glad our carriage came up in time to see this, it looked so pretty.

After a rest I took a walk with the German lady [Baroness de Grancy] and had more rest before tea, so I was not at all tired for dinner. The Queen called me up before going in to dinner and thanked me for my letter and beautiful cover, so at any rate she did get it, but I feel all the time I need not have sent it. We have had a ladies' dinner and all easy.

The Queen looks more marvellously well than ever. Such a good colour and not a bit weary or tired. One can't believe she is eighty. I am now going to my bed and hope not to be too cold. There are hot pipes in the passages but in the dining and drawing-room it was *bitterly* cold, but if I don't catch cold it may brace me.

Ever your loving grateful
Mother

P.S. Very good night darling and not cold. Glorious sunny morning. Post goes at nine. Always thinking of my beloved Con.

May 29

The winter look on grass, trees and everything, and sprouts only just beginning is rather trying, and they say they had not seen any sun till the day we came, and like March with us, rain is much wanted and the farmers are full of complaints over last year and the prospects of this one. The [day]light going on till nine is strange but delightful.

Yesterday there was no chapel here, and I did not fancy going alone to the Scotch Church much when Aline was taken for walk with the Queen, but wish I had done so as the Princesses Beatrice, Thora and Ena were alone, and the Queen rather expected me to go which I did not guess and no one suggested.

The greatest novelty here is the electric light, and it brightens up one's bedroom very much, but the Queen does not like it and feels glare very much for her eyes, and in the sitting-room it is not very skilfully done as there is a huge burner at the top which makes such a glare on the ceiling instead of having little lights round the top of the room, the daylight going on till 9 p.m. is very nice, and no shutters are shut, so one can watch the evening effects from the rooms.

The first night at dinner the Queen told us there was to be a fresh Dreyfus Court Martial she had just heard which seemed great news;[1] but last night there was nothing amusing; and

---

[1] It was not until June 3 that the united Appeal Courts gave their judgement which was that there had been a miscarriage of justice and that Dreyfus was to be retried by Court Martial, to be held at Rennes in order to avoid a demonstration in Paris.

the prospects of the time here are generally dull, but for the presence of dear Gerry Liddell.[1]

The Grand Duchess's little girl of four is such a pet. She has just gone out in a donkey chair accompanied by three people.

[This little girl, Elizabeth, was the only child of the Grand Duke and Duchess of Hesse. After her parents' divorce in 1901 she spent six months of the year with each of them. She died very suddenly in the autumn of 1903 while on a visit with her father to the Tsar and Tsarina in Poland. The circumstances of her death were mysterious. Some said she died of meningitis, others of para-typhoid, while at the time there was a rumour that she had been poisoned by a dish intended for the Tsar. Her parents had never been happy together but they both made successful second marriages in 1905, and had more children. Ducky married another first cousin, on her mother's side this time, the Grand Duke Cyril, first cousin of the Tsar; while Ernest married Elinore of Solms-Hohensolms-Lich.]

May 30

I drove with the Queen and Princess Thora yesterday afternoon, and it was lovely and warm, and soon after the start the Queen gave me a little case "as a remembrance" and it contained the little pendant she is giving her ladies with cypher of crown and "80" each side and crown with red enamel and one or two diamonds, and it is very pretty but too small for show. I kissed her Majesty's hand and thanked very much, and from herself it is extra nice to receive, so I was very pleased. We had tea by the Bridge of Dee and the Grand Duchess and Princess Ena who were riding met us there, and there was chaff and no stiffness. We had passed the little four-year-old Princess in the pony carriage, and she said, "Thank you dear Granma for lending me these ponies," and she offered the Queen a peppermint which she took and enjoyed. We were not in till seven but there was no chill and it was lovely weather.

[1] Geraldine Liddell was a great friend of Princess Thora.

Friday, 31

The Queen received all the servants and gave Checketts [Lady Lytton's maid] a nice fitted box with her own hand. Checketts could not sleep for thinking of the honour and was inclined to cry. I drove with the Queen and thanked her. We had tea at the Dantzig Lodge. Prince Maurice [of Battenberg] was so excited at fishing with the Grand Duchess.

Princess Beatrice told us she had lately had a letter from a man saying the Queen ought to wear a tight leather jacket, and have a little balloon easily puffed out, attached to it, which would drag her about easily as her knees are stiff. What a picture could be made of this.

Ever your
Mother

[We now come to the last passages of Lady Lytton's diary written at Osborne in August. The South African War was not two months away when she arrived there, but as yet the British Government was still hoping that President Kruger would grant the enfranchisement for which the Uitlanders were clamouring.]

15 *August* 1899

Lovely very hot day arrived at Osborne—nice tea out under the tree. The Connaughts, Princess Christian and Princess Thora made a large merry party. Band in the evening so only spoke to the Queen a few minutes after dinner. Felt very well with the change and not sleepy. Each day was lovely and sitting out under the cedar so very pleasant.

Wednesday, August 16

Drove with the Queen and she and Princess Christian talked so cheerfully and happily. The sunset was perfectly beautiful with scarlet red green blue sky and grey cloud effects.

August 17

A fête at Carisbrooke. Went with the Queen and Princess Thora going there, and through Newport there were a good many people. The sports were quite uninteresting and we only stayed twenty minutes. I came back with Harriet Phipps and Fanny Lambart.

[The object of the fête was to raise funds for the restoration of St Thomas's Church, Newport, which was under the Queen's patronage. The sports consisted of a "cycling gymkhana," one of the items of which was a "bill posting" competition, open to both ladies and gentlemen. The competitors had to ride up to a swinging board, paste their bills on the board and ride back to the starting place. This competition was said to have made Her Majesty smile very much.]

August 18

Lord Pauncefote [Sir Julian had been raised to the peerage that year] and Sir Claude MacDonald[1] were interesting diplomatists to meet. There was a loud military band in the evening.

August 19

Went with the Queen on board the *Victoria and Albert* and for a nice cruise to the sea and Hurst Castle[2] and saw the Needle rocks and had a good fresh breeze, but it was very hot. The sun setting a glowing red ball and streak along the water of fire was very beautiful.

Albani and Rumford sang beautifully in the evening and it is always so luxurious to sit comfortably in a drawing-room with good music.

Sunday, August 20

Quiet very hot sultry day. The Bishop of Sierra Leone preached well but stiffly twice. He felt a call to go out to

[1] Minister at Pekin. Ten months later he and the other foreign Ministers at Pekin were besieged in their Legations by the Boxers.

[2] Built by Henry VIII in 1539. Here Charles I was brought as a prisoner from Carisbrooke Castle and kept until he was taken to London for his trial.

10

Sierra Leone years ago and has had much fever and looks very weak but will go out again.[1] Evening service nice.

Monday, August 21

Very chilly. Had a walk with Aline to the sea. Admiral Seymour [Sir Michael Culme-Seymour, Admiral at Portsmouth] and General Sir Baker Russell [Commanding at Portsmouth] and the Cochranes[2] to tea. Table so lovely with yellow alamanders [sic] and very good Portsmouth Band—so cheerful and nice. Ill with colic at night, luckily after I got upstairs, went on till one—then a little in the morning.

August 22

Rather chilly early. Did not go out till after lunch, then all right. Drove with the Queen and Princess Thora to dear Ryde. The Queen spoke of Sir Robert Peel having helped to get Osborne property and Hall. Has made note to that effect on his bust in the corridor, and Osborne has been such a favourite place for them all always, Princess Beatrice being married here and her dear husband being buried here and she Governor of the Island has many links with it.[3] Such laughter as we went into Ryde at the maids being vexed when the Queen's new hat made at Windsor was put in the illustrated papers as a bonnet.

Ryde was quite the same as ever and filled me with old memories. Quiet ladies' dinner.

August 23

Lovely clear weather, fresh east wind. The Duke and Duchess of Connaught and party left at one. Conger eel to

[1] The Rt Rev. John Taylor Smith, born 1860, was Bishop of Sierra Leone from 1897 to 1901. He then became Chaplain General to the Army. In 1906 he was created C.V.O.

[2] Colonel and Lady Adela Cochrane. He was Deputy Governor of the Isle of Wight. They lived at Quarr Abbey, Ryde, where Princess Beatrice had spent her short honeymoon. The house had been lent by Colonel Cochrane's father, Sir Thomas Cochrane, who was also the father of Princess Beatrice's Lady-in-Waiting, Miss Minnie Cochrane.

[3] Princess Beatrice was made Governor of the Isle of Wight after Prince Henry's death. Sir Robert Peel, while he was Prime Minister, had first suggested the purchase of Osborne.

look at before lunch five feet long, was said to bark in the
water and kills other fish.

Princess Christian and Thora left at nine and took leave
of the Queen after tea. Mary Hughes and I drove with the
Queen by the sea. A man rushed at the carriage and threw in
a letter just before the Lodge. A German photographer but
[it] is a grave offence. Last man got two years. Sat by the
Queen at dinner but all easy and pleasant.

August 24

Very broiling hot, east wind and not very pleasant. After
lunch took in to the Queen Superintendent Nurse from
Madras and three nurses from the Niger, East Africa.
Her Majesty so gracious. Gave Orders. Lord Salisbury
arrived at 3.30. Heard of Sir James Reid's engagement to
Susan Baring, great surprise but he seems so happy.

[One is glad to know that at least one romance took place
at Court in spite of the Queen's disapproval of girls marrying.
Susan Baring, a daughter of the first Lord Revelstoke and
sister of Maurice Baring, was a Maid of-Honour to the Queen.
In the draft of a letter to Princess Christian, giving her
details of Lady Salisbury's illness, information for which she
had apparently asked, Lady Lytton wrote: "We were all so
surprised on Thursday to hear of Sir James Reid's engage-
mant to Susan Baring, and it is upsetting to the Queen though
it is hoped there will be no change in his residence, but one
hardly understands how this can be. Sir James seems very happy
and the household full of jokes and chaff." The Queen was
said to have been so angered by the engagement that she
would not see the doctor for three days, but when she did
eventually see him, he won her round at once by promising
never to do it again. Her objection to her courtiers marrying
was based on the belief that a man told his wife everything.
Susan Baring had been a Maid-of-Honour just over a year.
She went to Osborne for her first waiting on 18 August 1898,
and it was Lady Lytton who brought her to the Queen in a
tent in the garden. She knelt down and the Queen gave her

her badge—a scarlet ribbon bow—and a miniature of herself as a young woman, set in diamonds.]

I sat by Lord Salisbury at dinner but he talked to the Queen most of the time. In the evening I got more talk and made him sit down behind the Queen. Dear Lady Salisbury can read, he says, and remembers old times and is longing to get out in the air, which they hope may soon be possible, and if she could be moved to Hatfield he thinks she would be much more comfortable there.[1] Lord S. saw a letter from Lister [Secretary of Embassy at Paris] saying Dreyfus would probably just by a shave be let off. I wonder? Kruger will go on for his own people pretending not to give in but will not go to war as it would put an end to himself.

The drawing-room was very hot and for a few minutes the Queen was very sleepy which I have never seen at night.

[On September 9 Dreyfus was condemned by the Rennes Court Martial by five votes to two and sentenced to ten years' detention. The Queen heard the news on the same day from Mr Herbert, Secretary of Embassy in Paris, and sent back the following telegram: "Thanks for your telegram with the news of this monstrous verdict against this poor martyr. I trust he will appeal against this dreadful sentence." Her telegram was not in cypher; it leaked out in Paris and gave rise to the most terrible abuse of England and the Queen in the papers.

M. Loubet, the French President, gave him a free pardon on September 19 but it was not until July, 1906, that another Appeal Court quashed the verdict of the Rennes Court Martial and he was reinstated. Even then he was shabbily treated. He had refused any monetary indemnity and was merely decorated with the Legion of Honour, 4th grade,

---

[1] Lord Salisbury was Lord Warden of the Cinque Ports, and Lady Salisbury was staying at Walmer Castle, Dover, the Lord Warden's official house. Early in July she had had a slight stroke which had paralysed her left arm, and she was also still suffering from dropsy. She died at the end of November. Her fourth son, Lord Edward Cecil, was second in command of the garrison at Mafeking at the time, and Lady Edward (afterwards Viscountess Milner) tells us in her memoirs that the enemy allowed a native runner bearing news of her death to pass through their lines.

THE QUEEN, THE PRINCE OF WALES, THE DUKE OF YORK
AND PRINCE EDWARD

and promoted to the rank of Major which he would have attained in 1903 in the normal course of his career.]

August 25

Intensely hot early, cool later. South-west wind. Only sitting out and walk to the sea after tea with Fräulein Bauer who is so nice and chats so well. Sat by Lord Salisbury at dinner but the Queen talked all the time to him, but I had some talk again in the evening. He seemed to feel worrying herself had brought on Lady Salisbury's illness again, and the doctors are all so puzzled. Talking of Abyssinia, Lord Salisbury said the laws of marriage were so severe that they were afraid to marry and therefore dispensed with that ceremony. Lord Salisbury sat down so near the Queen that it was very awkward.

August 26

Lovely very hot day. I felt rather seedy after medicine and no relief so wrote in my room after sitting out a little. There were sports in the Field for the Prince Consort's birthday, and after the two o'clock dinner his health is drunk in silence. I went with the Queen and Harriet to the sports, and back with Princess Beatrice to give away the prizes, and the Queen asked the people to dance and she watched it with pleasure, and when Niggers sang she thought she ought to leave.

It was quite hot driving even at seven. A nice band in the evening and some people to dinner. The Queen sent me a group of the four generations—her Majesty, the Prince of Wales, Duke of York and Prince Edward, all so like only I don't like the Queen photographed in her hat. The Page said the Queen wished me to have it on the 26th, to her such a special day.

Sunday, August 27

Hot morning, south-west gale and cool after. Aline and I took a walk after Chapel. Evening Church. Ladies' dinner always nice and the Queen very cheery talking in the evening of maids-of-honour and ladies of old times.

Here the diary ends, and it is pleasant to leave the Queen chatting cheerily of old days. She had seventeen more months to live. Twice again the dreadful December 14 was to come round, and on the last of them in 1900 she wrote, "This sad day, so full of terrible memories, returned again." It was the thirty-ninth anniversary of the Consort's death. And there was to be one more August 26 when she wrote: "This ever dear day has returned again without my beloved Albert being with me, who, on this day, eighty-one years ago, came into the world as a blessing to so many, leaving an imperishable name behind him! How I remember the happy day it used to be, and preparing presents for him, which he would like! . . . All, all is engraven on my mind and in my heart!"

In those last months of her life she had much sorrow. Lord Salisbury had been too sanguine as to the chances of peace. On October 12 the Boers, after issuing an ultimatum that was impossible for the British Government to accept, invaded the British Colonies, and the whole of the rest of her life was clouded by this terrible conflict, the worst war England had yet known, which dragged on month after month. And then on 31 July 1900 her second son Alfred, Duke of Coburg, died of cancer. She was indignant that the truth about his illness had been withheld from her, for now his death came as such a terrible shock. "Oh, God! my poor darling Affie gone too!" she cried in her journal. "My third grown-up child, besides three very dear sons-in-law.[1] It is hard at eighty-one! . . . one sorrow, one trial, one anxiety, following another. It is a horrible year, nothing but sadness and horrors of one kind and another."

But even more tragedy was to come. Prince Christian Victor, always called Christle, the elder son of Prince and Princess Christian, who was A.D.C. to Lord Roberts, died on October 28 of enteric at Pretoria on the eve of coming home. He was only thirty-three.[2]

[1] Princess Alice died 1878; Leopold, Duke of Albany, the Queen's youngest son who suffered from haemophilia, 1884; the Emperor Frederick 1888; the Duke of Hesse 1892, and Prince Henry of Battenberg 1896.

[2] An account of his death in a letter from Lady Lytton is given in Appendix J on p. 168.

The Queen's Death 151

The Queen's wonderful health broke down at last in November 1900 while she was at Windsor. There was so much sadness, and now she was desperately anxious about her eldest daughter, the Empress Frederick, who, suffering terribly, was bedridden and could no longer use her hands.

The Queen never felt well after that; she lost her appetite; she could not sleep at night and then would fall asleep in the morning just as she wanted to get up which she described as "most provoking," the strongest adjective she ever used about her own infirmities. In spite of feeling so ill she continued to carry out her duties, welcoming troops from South Africa, receiving Lord Ampthill, who was going out to Madras as Governor and creating him a G.C.S.I., attending a sale of needlework at Windsor Town Hall (her last public appearance), reading State papers and signing documents.

She went to Osborne on December 18 but she was getting weaker. Princess Beatrice and Princess Christian had to write her letters, and her favourite grand-daughter, Thora, her journal. She was not allowed to die, though, without one more terrible blow. On Christmas Day her old friend Jane Churchill, who was in waiting, died of heart failure. She had been with her nearly fifty years and was her oldest and most intimate friend. In March 1899 the Queen had written: "All fall around me, and I have become more and more lonely." She must have felt even more lonely now.

She did not survive Lady Churchill a month. On Tuesday, 22 January 1901, at 6.45 P.M. she died. Four days after her death Fritz Ponsonby wrote to Lady Lytton from Osborne: "I am only so thankful that she died in harness as she wished, hard at work till the last moment and that she did not have to resign the throne and have a Regency instead. That would have been such a sad end to her splendid life. . . The behaviour of the new King and Queen has been beyond all words. They both hate coming to the Throne. He said twenty years ago he would have liked it immensely but now he had settled down to his life and he had not the slightest wish to reign.

The Princess of Wales refuses to be called Queen as she says that at present there can only be one Queen and she wishes to remain Princess of Wales until after the funeral. It is all very difficult and the two households get very much mixed, and no one knows who is who."

Lady Lytton was to have gone into waiting, succeeding Lady Ampthill, on the very day the Queen died, but a few days beforehand she received a telegram from Princess Christian putting her off as the house was full of those members of the Royal Family who had rushed to Osborne on hearing how seriously ill the Queen was. Lady Lytton replied that "should it be God's will that the Queen should not recover, I pray your Royal Highness that I may be allowed to go and take my farewell of her Majesty and the truest and best friend we have ever had." Her prayer was answered, and shortly after the Queen's death she was summoned to Osborne by an undated telegram signed by Harriet Phipps. And in a letter dated January 28 Miss Phipps wrote to her: "I am so glad you are coming. There will be a vacant room for you on Wednesday [the younger members of the Royal Family were leaving Osborne on that day, the 30th]. You and I have the great privilege of attending our most beloved Queen on her last journey. *Orders* are difficult to obtain but what I, with Charlotte Knollys's advice, have got is a cashmere dress with a deep band of crape on the skirt and deep crape on the bodice, white lawn collars and cuffs—a *crape* bonnet with a long crape veil at the back nearly to the ground, and of course a deep veil over the face. Then for the nights at Windsor we should wear little crape points with equally long veil at back for dinner! foreign fashion. The evening dresses are just the same as the day—only longer skirts. Of course one's outdoor wraps should be deep also. I write all this just from *me* to *you*, dearest. They are only for your convenience as it is difficult to get what is needed in haste and it may help you."

Lady Lytton did not arrive until after the coffin was nailed down, but she prayed by it and "tried to feel the peace for her Majesty," as she noted on an odd scrap of paper. On the evening of Friday, February 1, she crossed with the coffin to

THE LAST PHOTOGRAPH OF LADY LYTTON
BEFORE HER RETIREMENT

Portsmouth on the *Alberta*, while the new King and the other mourners followed on the *Victoria and Albert*, and, in her own words, scribbled at the top of Miss Phipps's letter, "was alone with Harriet by the Queen's coffin and five admirals." She and Harriet slept that night on the *Osborne* in Portsmouth Harbour, and on Saturday morning accompanied the coffin by train to Victoria Station, the other mourners having gone on ahead in another special train.

In after years Lady Lytton used to tell her grandchildren how in the early morning, sitting by the coffin in the train with the blinds down, she peeped out and saw the Queen's subjects kneeling beside the track as the train went by.

Lady Lytton herself had a much happier old age. She became as devoted to Queen Alexandra as she had been to Victoria, but in 1905 she retired from Court to a small newly-built house at Knebworth, called Homewood, about two miles from the big house, given to her by her son Victor and designed by her son-in-law, Edwin Lutyens, and there she lived until her death, at the age of ninety-five, in October 1936. Her daughter Constance, who never married, lived with her. Constance became a militant suffragette in 1908 and went four times to prison. Lady Lytton minded this dreadfully and looked upon it as a family disgrace, but when Constance had a stroke in 1912 as the result of forcible feeding in prison and became an invalid for the rest of her life (she died in 1923), her mother devoted herself exclusively to looking after her with the greatest tenderness.

But apart from this one great sorrow, Lady Lytton was very happy and lived to see twenty-four great-grandchildren, the youngest of whom, twin girls, were born on her own birthday a month before her death.

She slipped contentedly into second-childhood. Her memory had completely gone at the end—she did not even recognise her own children—but her health was splendid and she never lost her exquisite manners, her dignity or her charm.

She and I had always been very special friends, and it made me very sad when she did not recognise me at the end. The last time I saw her I said to her, "But, Granny, don't you really remember me? I'm Mary. I used to have long plaits and sit on the window-sill over there."

"Oh, yes," she replied, "I knew *her intimately.*" And then she added wistfully, "But she never comes to see me now."

Appendix A

QUEEN VICTORIA AND HER CHILDREN

Part of a letter from Queen Victoria to Queen Augusta of Prussia, whose son the Crown Prince Frederick had just become engaged to the Queen's eldest daughter. Princess Victoria was only fifteen when she became engaged, but she waited to get married until she was seventeen.

Balmoral, October 6, 1856.

I see the children much less & even here, where Albert is often away all day long, I find no special pleasure or compensation in the company of the elder children. You will remember that I told you this at Osborne. Usually they go out with me in the afternoon (Vicky mostly, & the others also sometimes), or occasionally in the mornings when I drive or walk or ride, accompanied by my lady-in-waiting, & only very occasionally do I find the rather intimate intercourse with them either agreeable or easy. You will not understand this, but it is caused by various factors. Firstly, I only feel properly *à mon aise* & quite happy when Albert is with me; secondly, I am used to carrying on my many affairs quite alone; & then I have grown up all alone, accustomed to the society of adult (& never with younger) people —lastly, I still cannot get used to the fact that Vicky is almost grown up. To me she still seems the same child, who had to be kept in order & therefore must not become too intimate. Here are my sincere feelings in contrast to yours.[1]

[1] *Further Letters of Queen Victoria*, edited by Hector Bolitho.

Appendix B

A PRIVATE PRESENTATION

Emily, Lady Lytton's youngest daughter, was privately presented to the Queen at Windsor six months after her father's death. Lady Lytton wrote the following account of it:

Windsor expedition for Emmie's presentation,
May 16th, 1892.

Our arrival was quite grand. Dear Victor met us at the station, then we got into an open Landau with Postillion and pair.

On arrival at the Castle we were conducted to private rooms and told luncheon would be served for us alone. Miss Phipps soon came down, and was most kind, and she returned after luncheon also.

Sir Henry Ponsonby also came to speak about his son going to the Cape as A.D.C. to the Lochs[1] and was very nice though seemingly nervous.

At three the Queen received us in the little ante-room leading to her rooms. Her first look of intense compassion and gentle tender sympathy touched me very much, and she kissed Emily, gave her hand to Vic, and after saying he was like his father, she dismissed them, and asked me to sit down by her for about twenty minutes.

I talked of dear Robert as much as possible, and the family and all I could think of the Queen's sorrow, journeys etc. One time she said that sorrow changed one so much, at another, speaking of the letters, that it was a great mistake to publish anything personal said of other people. She said I had been such a good wife, and I answered that my dear husband had guided me in all things and in every detail. The Queen did not like Costebelle [Hyères] and found it very relaxing. The Emperor of Germany was now kinder to his mother she said.

It was a great honour to be privately presented to the Queen before marriage, but Emily's only recollections of the visit were her joy in being allowed for the first time to wear a bonnet (albeit a black one because they were still in mourning) which was a symbol that she was at last really grown-up; and the difficulty of getting at the right level to be kissed by the Queen: when she curtsied she was too low and when she stood up too high.

[1] Lord Loch, Lady Lytton's brother-in-law, was Governor of the Cape from 1889 to 1895. It was Sir Henry Ponsonby's eldest son, John, who became his A.D.C.

Appendix C

LETTER FROM THE QUEEN
TO THE NATION

(From the *London Gazette*)

WHITEHALL, February 15, 1896.

The following letter from The Queen has been received by the Right Honourable the Secretary of State for the Home Department:

Osborne, February 14, 1896.

I have, alas! once more to thank My loyal subjects for their warm sympathy in a fresh grievous affliction which has befallen Me and My beloved Daughter, Princess Beatrice, Princess Henry of Battenberg.

This new sorrow is overwhelming, and to Me is a double one, for I lose a dearly loved and helpful Son, whose presence was like a bright sunbeam in My Home, and My dear Daughter loses a noble devoted Husband to whom she was united by the closest affection.

To witness the blighted happiness of the Daughter who has never left Me, and has comforted and helped Me, is hard to bear. But the feeling of universal sympathy so touchingly shown by all classes of My subjects has deeply moved My Child and Myself, and has helped and soothed us greatly. I wish from My heart to thank My people for this, as well as for the appreciation manifested of the dear and gallant Prince who laid down his life in the service of his adopted Country.

My beloved Child is an example to all, in her courage, resignation, and submission to the will of God.

VICTORIA, R.I.

Lord James of Hereford wrote in his diary on February 15: "Sir Arthur Bigge told me that the Queen's beautiful letter of thanks to her people on the death of Prince Henry was written by the Queen (notwithstanding her failing sight) by her own hand, without making one correction. She had no assistance in its composition."

The Queen herself wrote in her journal on February 14: "Wrote a letter to be published in the papers, thanking my people for their kind sympathy with Beatrice and me in our great sorrow."

To mark Prince Henry's death, the Queen instituted, on 21 April 1896, the Royal Victorian Order "as a reward for personal services to the Queen and her successors." It is in the sole gift of the Sovereign.

Appendix D

ANNOUNCING AN ENGAGEMENT

Below is a letter from Nicholas to his mother, the Empress Marie Feodorovna, describing his engagement. The original was written in Russian. In Russia the Julian Calendar was still kept. It was twelve days behind the rest of Europe (thirteen days after 1900), and therefore this letter is dated April 10, two days after the engagement.[1]

Palais Edinburg in Koburg,
10th April, 1894.

My dear Beloved Mama,

I don't know how to begin this letter. I want to see you so much, but my thoughts are somehow quite confused. This is how, with God's merciful help, my quest which seemed to me so desperate found its fulfilment. The day after I came here I had a long and very difficult talk with Alix, in which I tried to explain to her that there was no other way for her than to give her consent, and that she simply could not withhold it. She cried the whole time, and only whispered now and then, "No, I cannot!" Still I went on, repeating and insisting on what I had said before. And though this talk went on for two hours it came to nothing; because neither she nor I would give in. The next morning we talked in a much calmer way. I gave her your letter, and after that she couldn't argue any more. This already was a kind of proof to me of the final struggle which had been going on in her from the time of our first talk. The marriage of Erni and Ducky was the measure of her sorrow and indecision. She decided to have a talk with Aunt Michen,[1] and was supported in this by Erni. He gave me to understand that there was hope of everything ending well. About myself I must say that during those three days I was in a state of painful anxiety. All the relatives one after another asked me about her, with their best wishes for me; in a word, they were very touching in their

---

[1] All the Roman Catholic countries adopted Pope Gregory's Calendar in 1582. Great Britain and her dominions, including the North American colonies, did not adopt it until 1752; Soviet Russia adopted it in 1917, and the Russian Church in 1923.

[2] The Grand Duchess Marie Pavlovna, a German Princess married to Nicholas's uncle, the Grand Duke Vladimir. She also had had to change her faith.

solicitude. But this made me even more afraid of something evil happening. The Emperor [William] did what he could; he even had a talk with Alix, and brought her that morning—the 8th April—to our house. Then she went to Aunt Michen again and, soon after, joined us in the room where we were sitting with the Uncles and Aunt Ella[1] and Wilhelm. We were left alone, and with her very first words she consented! The Almighty only knows what happened to me then. I cried like a child and she did too; but her expression had changed; her face was lit up by a quiet content. No, dear Mama, I can't tell you how happy I am and how sad at the same time that I am not with you and can't take you and dearest Papa to my heart at this moment. The whole world is changed for me: nature, mankind, everything; and all seem to be good and lovable and happy. I couldn't even write, my hands trembled so, and indeed I hadn't a second to myself. I had to do what all the rest of the family were doing. I had to answer *hundreds* of telegrams, though what I really wanted all the time was to be sitting alone in a quiet corner with my dear fiancée. She is quite changed. She is gay and amusing and talkative and *tender*. I can't thank God enough for his mercy. We had a *Te Deum* the same day in Aunt Marie's[2] church. She [Alix] and all her sisters attended too. By Alix's wish we are going to Darmstadt for the night. Now she will see her home with quite different feelings. I intended to be away for two weeks, but I now think of returning earlier, about the middle of Easter week. I want so much to be with her a little longer.

And now, my dear Mama, I have to come to an end. I enclose her letter to you. Love to dear Papa and you all. Your

NICKY

[1] Alix's sister who had married Nicholas's uncle the Grand Duke Serge.
[2] The Duchess of Coburg (Edinburgh).

Appendix E

LETTERS OF THE TSAR AND TSARINA

The Tsar and Tsarina always wrote to each other in English, but the Tsar's letters published in England are translated from the Russian text, the only one available. Thus we have the translation of a translation which is bound to differ from the original English version, so it is impossible to know how well he really wrote English. The Tsarina's letters are ungrammatical and badly spelt, but one cannot help feeling that it is the editing which is mostly at fault.[1] The Tsar's are much more carefully edited and in quite good English. The Tsar always remembered his wedding day in his letters, but it was the day of their engagement that was their most precious anniversary. In accordance with the Julian calendar this anniversary fell on April 8. On that day, in 1915, he wrote to his wife from the Front:

My precious Darling,

My warm and loving thanks for your dear letter, full of tender words, and for both telegrams. I too have you in my thoughts on this our 21st anniversary! I wish you health and all that a deeply loving heart can desire, and thank you on my knees for all your love, affection, friendship and patience, which you have shown me during these long years of our married life!

And a year later, still at the Front, he wrote on April 7:

Tomorrow is the 8th; my prayers and thoughts will be with you, my girl, my own Sunny. At that time I fought for you, even against yourself! ! !
Like the little Boy Blue, only more stubbornly.[2]

And on the 8th:

MY DEAR BELOVED,

I must begin my letter to-day with reminiscences of what happened 22 years ago! As far as I remember, there was a Concert

---

[1] It is the Slovo edition of her letters, published in Berlin, which was printed in England in 1923.
[2] Little Boy Blue is the nickname of the hero of *Through the Postern Gate* by Florence Barclay, author of *The Rosary*. The Tsar had read this novel in March and had been greatly impressed by it. It was published in 1912 and sold two hundred thousand copies.

in Coburg that evening and a Bavarian band was playing; poor Uncle Alfred [the Duke of Coburg] was rather exhausted by dinner, and constantly dropped his stick with a clatter. Do you remember? ... My beloved, I want you very much ... good-night, my dear beloved darling.

The Tsarina wrote to him on these two anniversaries from the Alexander Palace at Tsarskoe Selo.

April 7th, 1915.

My very own sweet One,

Every possible tender wish for to-morrow. The first time in 21 years we don't spend this anniversary together.—How vividly one remembers all! Ah, my beloved Boy, what happiness and love you have given me all these years—God verily richly blessed our married life. For all your wify thanks you from the depths of her big loving heart. May God Almighty make me a worthy helpmate of yours, my own sweet treasure, my sunshine, Sunbeam's[1] Father!

And on the 8th:

My very own beloved husband,

Tenderly do my prayers and grateful thoughts linger around you this dear anniversary! How the years go by! 21 years already! You know I have kept the grey princess dress I wore that morning? And shall wear your dear brooch. Dear me, how much we have lived through together in these years—heavy trials everywhere, but at home in our nest, bright sunshine!

And the next year on the 8th she wrote:

My own sweet Nicky love,

On this our engagement day all my tenderest thoughts are with you, filling my heart with boundless gratitude for the intense love and happiness you have given me ever since that memorable day, 22 years ago. May God help me to repay you hundredfold for all your sweetness.

Yes, verily I doubt there being such happy wives as I am—such love, trust and devotion as you have shown me these long years with happiness and sorrow. All the anguish, suffering and indecision have been well worth what I received from you, my precious bridegroom and husband. Now-a-days one rarely sees such marriages. Your wonderful patience and forgiveness are untold—I can only ask God Almighty on my knees to bless and repay you for everything—He alone can. Thank you, Sweetheart and feel

---

[1] The Tsarevitch, Alexis, born in 1904, was often referred to as Sunbeam.

my longing to be held in your arms tightly clasped and to relive our beautiful bridal days, which daily brought new tokens of love and sweetness. That dear brooch will be worn to-day. I feel still your grey suit, the smell of it by the window in the Coburg Schloss. How vivid I remember everything; those sweet kisses which I had dreamed of and yearned after so many years and which I thought I should never get. You see, as even then, faith and religion play a strong part in my life. I cannot take this simply—and when make up for sure mind, then it's already for always—the same in my love and affection. A far too big heart which eats me up. And the love for Christ too—and it has always been so closely linked with our lives these 22 years. First the question of taking the orthodox faith and then our two friends sent to us by God. . . . Yes, me loves oo, my Little Boy Blue and already 31 years and belong to you 22.

It is clear from this letter that she had loved him as long as he had loved her—since she was twelve. The two friends she refers to are Philippe, a French mystic, and Rasputin. When Philippe was banished he prophesied that another man of God would be sent to her.

Mossilov, head of the Court Chancery between 1900 and 1916, tells us that part of the ritual of conversion to the Orthodox religion included the act, instituted in the middle ages, of "spitting thrice on the ground" in evidence of contempt for the religion that is to be renounced, a practice that might well hold anyone back from changing his faith, let alone someone as sincerely devout as Alix. It seems, though, that this part of the ceremony was omitted from Alix's conversion.

Appendix F

THE TSAR'S ACCOUNT OF BALMORAL

From the letter given below, written to his mother, it is evident that Nicholas did not enjoy his stay at Balmoral, but although he was thankful for the respite from shooting while the Prince of Wales was away at Newmarket, he did in fact adore shooting, and one wonders whether his failure to get a stag, "though in the best place" as Lady Lytton tells us, soured him a little. (According to a letter from the Empress to her old governess he shot only one brace of grouse during the entire visit.) When there was nothing else to shoot he used to shoot crows in the park of his own palace, and record the bag in his diary.

Balmoral Castle, 13th September [Julian calendar], 1896.

About 10 in the morning we entered the roadstead of Leith. Strong wind and rain. The Channel Squadron was anchored there; we passed quite close by it. At 11 a.m. the steamer with Uncle Bertie and Uncle Arthur and the English suite arrived. We had about two hours before going on shore, and so we gave them lunch. I wore the Scots Greys' uniform with bearskin—you will understand how unpleasant it was to have to say good-bye to our officers and crew in foreign uniform! Big reception in a tent on the quay, where the Mayors of Leith and Edinburgh met us presenting addresses. After that a procession to the town, escorted by the Scots Greys: in open carriages, under pouring rain all the way.

At a quarter past two the train left, and not till 7 did it reach its destination, Ballater, where Georgie and May were waiting. We were greeted with addresses at every station along the line, just as when we landed. The train was rather rocky so that Alix was very nearly ill, but Baby, thank God, was none the worse and was quite fresh and jolly when we arrived at Balmoral at about 8 o'clock. Granny was waiting for us on the steps with the family and the household. I didn't think her much changed except that she seemed a little smaller—just as you found her. Again she is marvellously kind and amiable to us, and so delighted to see our little daughter! From the very first day my Uncles took charge of me. They seem to think it necessary to take me out shooting all day long with the gentlemen. The weather is awful, rain and wind every day and on top of it no luck at all—I haven't killed a stag yet. I see even less of

Alix here than at home, where deputations and audiences with Ministers interfere enough.

The account of his visit was continued in a letter dated October 2 and written from Darmstadt, where he and Alix went after their visit to France. He apologised for not writing for a fortnight and then continued:

To begin with, I would like to tell you a little about the end of our stay at Balmoral. The weather improved in the last few days. Uncle Bertie left with Worontsoff and Dima [Galitzin] for Newmarket where one of his horses again won a race. After he left I had an easier time, because I could at least do what I wanted to, and was *not* obliged to go out shooting every day in the cold and rain. We went to Mar Lodge and had lunch with all the family at Louise's. There for the first time we met Maud and Carl [of Denmark]—it seems rather strange for them to be husband and wife. Granny was kinder and more amiable than ever. She sent Lord Salisbury to see me, and I had two very serious talks with him. It's good at least for him to learn from the source what the opinions and views of Russia are. From Balmoral to Portsmouth we were given Granny's own very comfortable railway carriage. We were taken right up to the *Polar Star*, which was moored to the quay, and had dinner with all the English Admirals and Generals. Next day we left at 7 in the morning, and arrived at Cherbourg at 2 p.m. We could, of course, have crossed in much better time, but were held up by the English and French squadrons conveying us. An interesting and beautiful sight was the meeting of the two squadrons in mid-channel. Our yacht and all the other ships rolled considerably; a gale was blowing and the seas were very high. Alix was ill and our poor little girl too; even I was rather sick once.

The rest of the letter is an account of the visit to Paris which he enjoyed far more than his stay at Balmoral. Little Olga also seems to have been very happy there. "Our daughter made a great impression everywhere. The first thing in the morning Faure [the President] asked Alix about was the health 'of the little Grand Duchess.' Everybody in the streets greeted her with 'long live the Grand-duchess!' which she apparently liked very much, because she laughed all the time."

Appendix G

THE CAIRN

In *Leaves from the Journal of our Life in the Highlands* the Queen describes the building of the Cairn to commemorate the purchase of Balmoral:

Monday, October 11, 1852.

This day has been a very happy, lucky and memorable one—our last! A fine morning . . . it was nearly eleven o'clock before we could go up to the top of Craig Gowan, to see the cairn built, which was to commemorate our taking possession of this dear place; the old cairn having been pulled down. We set off with all the children, ladies, gentlemen and a few servants, including Macdonald and Grant, who had not already gone up; and at the Moss House, which is half way, Mackay met us, and preceded us, playing, Duncan and Donald Stewart[1] going before him, to the highest point of Craig Gowan; where were assembled all the servants and tenants, with their wives and children and old relations. . . .

I then placed the first stone, after which Albert laid one, then the children, according to their ages. All the ladies and gentlemen placed one; and then everyone came forward at once, each person carrying a stone and placing it on the cairn. . . . Mackay played and whiskey was given to all. It took, I am sure, an hour building; and whilst it was going on, some merry reels were danced on a stone opposite. All the old people danced; and many of the children. . . . At last, when the cairn, which is, I think, seven or eight feet high, was nearly completed, Albert climbed up to the top of it, and placed the last stone; after which three cheers were given. It was a gay, pretty and touching sight; and I felt almost inclined to cry. The view was so beautiful over the dear hills; the day so fine; the whole so *gemüthlich*. May God bless this place, and allow us yet to see it and enjoy it many a long year!

[1] Donald Stewart was the father of the head keeper Lady Lytton met at Balmoral. Duncan was another keeper and Grant the head keeper. Macdonald was Prince Albert's *Jäger*, while Mackay had been their piper since 1843. He went out of his mind in 1854 and died the following year.

Appendix H

G. F. WATTS ON NEVILLE LYTTON'S PORTRAITS

In February 1899 Lady Lytton arranged to show Neville's portraits of Edward Marsh and Ruth Balfour to G. F. Watts, then aged eighty-two, who was an old family friend. Eddie Marsh was present at the showing in Watts's Kensington studio and wrote to Neville in Paris describing it.

Ruth was shown first, and the first thing he said was that it was very French, but you had plenty of time to get out of that. Then my portrait appeared (which I will call E.). "Ah," he said, "he ought to do." Then he looked at them both and said, "Now R. is *better* than it is, but E. is more *promising*. R. couldn't be made better than it is, but E. shows that he sees the way to doing something of a better kind." Then he went on to say that the two men who became in the end more *de premier coup* than anyone else—Velasquez and Rembrandt—both began by painting very carefully and "tightly"— he said that Velasquez' earliest pictures were even tighter than E. and not so good! and that to paint like that at first was the surest way to get on. "I know what I say is true. I've been thinking about it for years." Then he began looking at Ruth again, and evidently thought it charming. "That's *beautiful*, I wouldn't have touched it for worlds," but that the difference was that you'd tried to do R. *cleverly* and had tried to do E. *well*—he evidently didn't think E. quite successful—he made a gesture-of-the hand in the neighbourhood of the cheek, and said, "All that doesn't matter," implying that it wasn't right—he said you hadn't tried to make a picture of it, and that that was quite right. I told him that all he'd been saying was really almost exactly what you thought yourself—and that you'd made up your mind not to do any more sketchy portraits but to take great pains and finish things.[1]

Edward Marsh in his own book of reminiscences, *A Number of People*, describes the picture of Ruth as "a lovely little thing, scumbled in grey and green and silver, with the look of an improvisation."

[1] This letter is taken from *Edward Marsh* by Christopher Hassall.

Appendix J

THE DEATH OF PRINCE CHRISTLE

Lady Lytton was at Balmoral when the news came on 29 October 1900 that Prince Christle had died at Pretoria of what was called "African fever." The next day she wrote to her twin sister, Lady Loch:

Balmoral Castle   October 30th [1900]   Tuesday, 6 p.m.

Well Beloved,

As Princess Thora was starting at five, she kissed me and said, "Do write to Lady Loch and thank her so much for her sympathy and tell her all." I then took her place in the Queen's carriage and had her [the Queen] to myself which was so much better and she quite sobbed and squeezed my hand. Oh, Lizey, it was so awful after lunch yesterday to hear the Prince had passed away and that Princess Thora was going herself to tell the Queen, but the Queen says she was wonderful and said, "Grandmama, he is gone." The news from Lord Roberts had been more anxious early but one could not help hoping, then all the afternoon was so black and dark but I heard nothing and had nothing to do. But when dressed for a Household dinner Princess Thora sent for me and she was lying on her bed such a picture of controlled misery, but she said, "His work was finished and he has had to give up," and told me of Lord Roberts's wire that he had passed peacefully away, and the Queen says Lord Roberts was with him to the last, but he had been semi-conscious since Saturday. Lord Kitchener had sent a very cordial wire saying he and the whole Army regretted the Prince who had a promising career before him. Princess Thora said he wished to lie where he died as the other soldiers did, so the Queen has consented to it. I knelt by Princess Thora after kissing her, and held her hand. I am glad she has gone to her mother and she has Gerry,[1] and they will meet the father at Buckingham Palace, But, Oh, what a changed home it will be, all their thoughts were so centred on this dear son as one can well understand.

The Household dinner last night was not too gloomy and I had Lord George Hamilton and Alick Yorke. To-night the ladies are to dine with the Queen and Princess Beatrice, and we must do our

---

[1] Geraldine Liddell, her great friend.

best to talk. I have just had ten telegrams to answer and I expect there will be more, and several have written to me round here. The Queen was able to get some sleep last night but breaking down after hearing the news helped her to sleep I am sure. Princess Thora also had some. I woke early with the horrid sense of loss to them all. It was so beloved of you to wire to the Queen also, darling, but they do so appreciate sympathy.

Windsor next Tuesday now, I am glad to say.

Ever your loving
EDES

The above letter, copied out by a maid whom Lady Lytton had in after years, was enclosed in her diary, and in the same handwriting was another page saying:

I heard later, the Prince received the Holy Communion when he was dying and Lord Roberts received with him and when he left the room he looked quite broken down and said, "My son over again."[2] The Prince when in his coffin with glass over the face was left in the church with a guard and two officers night and day, and there were short services and twice Holy Communion and about a thousand soldiers were allowed to pass and see him. The Prince asked for a writing desk and took out a letter from his Mother and one from Princess Thora and held the latter in his hand till he quietly passed away.

[2] In December 1899 Lord Roberts's only son had died of wounds received at the Battle of Colenso.

Biographical Index

of those mentioned in the book who are not listed in
readily available reference books.

Alexander, the Hon. Walter (1849–1934); Colonel Commanding
the Royal Scots Greys; 2nd son of the 3rd Earl of Caledon;
married in 1882 Margaret Katherine, who died 1929, daughter of
Rev. the Hon. Francis Grimston, son of the 1st Earl of Verulam.

Ampthill, Emily, *née* Villiers (1843–1927), the youngest of Lord
Clarendon's three daughters and Lady Lytton's first cousin.
In 1863 she married Lord Odo Russell, brother of the 9th Duke
of Bedford, who was created Baron Ampthill in 1881. He was for
twelve years *Chargé d'affaires* in Rome, and it was there that
Emily Villiers met him. He was sent on a special mission to Versailles during the 1870 war where he negotiated with Bismarck
the Black Sea Treaty. Bismarck took a great fancy to him and
asked that he should be made Ambassador in Berlin, which he was,
passing over the heads of many senior men. He remained in Berlin
from 1871–84 when he died. After his death Lady Ampthill
became a Lady-in-Waiting to Queen Victoria. Shortly before her
marriage she was a bridesmaid to the Princess of Wales (Queen
Alexandra).

Biddulph, Mary Fredericka, only daughter of Frederick Charles
Seymour and widow of Sir Thomas Biddulph, joint Keeper of the
Privy Purse, whom she married in 1857 and who died in 1878;
Maid-of-Honour to Queen Victoria 1850–56; Honorary Woman-
of-the-Bedchamber from 1857 until the Queen's death, and extra
Lady-in-Waiting to Princess Beatrice, as was also her daughter
Freda.

Borthwick, Algernon (1830–1908); in 1852 succeeded his father,
Peter Borthwick as editor of the *Morning Post*, and bought the
paper in 1876; Conservative M.P. for Kensington 1885–95. In
1887 he was created a Baronet and was raised to the peerage as
Baron Glenesk in 1895. In the same year he handed over control
of the *Morning Post* to his only son Oliver (1873–1905). He
married Alice Lister in 1870. For a time he edited a magazine
called the *Owl*. He was always keenly interested in the theatre.
He was one of the earliest members of the Primrose League,
founded in 1883. In London the Glenesks lived at 139 Piccadilly
where they did a great deal of entertaining. Towards the end of

his life he gave up shooting in Scotland owing to ill health, and divided his time between London and his villa at Cannes where he gave large house parties every winter. At his death the peerage became extinct.

Borthwick, Alice (1842–1899), younger daughter of Thomas Henry Lister and Lady Theresa Villiers, only sister of Lord Clarendon and of Lady Lytton's father. In 1870 she married Algernon Borthwick. Her only sister married Sir William Harcourt, and her only daughter Lord Bathhurst. She was the Vice-President of the Primrose League of which Lady Salisbury was the President.

Cadogan, the Hon. Ethel, born 1853, daughter of the Hon. Frederick William Cadogan and grand-daughter of the 3rd Earl Cadogan; Maid-of-Honour to Queen Victoria 1876–97 and Woman-of-the-Bedchamber 1897–1901.

Carington, the Hon. William, born 1845; Lieut.-Colonel Grenadier Guards; brother of Earl Carrington; Groom-in-Waiting and later Equerry to Queen Victoria 1880–1901; Comptroller to Edward VII 1901–10; Keeper of the Privy Purse to George V from 1910 until his death in 1914; K.C.V.O. 1901. In 1871 he married an American girl Juliet Warden, the daughter of Francis Warden.

Cazalet, William (1865–1932), only son of Edward Cazalet of Fairlawn; married in 1893 Maud Lucia, eldest daughter of Sir John Heron-Maxwell, 7th Bart. The Cazalets were merchants of Huguenot stock, and William Cazalet was one of the richest commoners in England. The family fortune had been made in Brazil.

Cecil, Lord William (1854–1943), 3rd son of the 3rd Marquess of Exeter; married in 1885 Mary, Baroness Amherst of Hackney in her own right, who died in 1919. He was a Groom-in-Waiting to Queen Victoria from 1892–1901, and then became Comptroller and Treasurer to Princess Beatrice.

Clinton, Lord Edward Pelham (1836–1907), second son of the 5th Duke of Newcastle; Colonel of the Rifle Brigade; Master of the Household to Queen Victoria 1894–1901, and Groom-in-Waiting to Edward VII; G.C.V.O. 1901. He married in 1865 Matilda Jane, who died 1892, daughter of Sir W. E. Cradock-Hartopp, Bart.

Cochrane, Annette Minna (Minnie), Lady-in-Waiting to Princess Beatrice. She was the daughter of Admiral of the Fleet Sir Thomas J. Cochrane and his second wife Rosetta, daughter of Sir Jonah Wheeler-Cuffe, Bart.

Cochrane, Colonel Thomas-Belhaven of Quarr Abbey, Ryde, son of Admiral Sir Thomas Cochrane and great-grandson of the 8th Earl of Dundonald. He was deputy Governor of the Isle of Wight and Captain of Carisbrooke Castle. He was a brother of

Miss Minnie Cochrane, Lady-in-Waiting to Princess Beatrice, and it was their father who had lent Quarr Abbey to Princess Beatrice for her honeymoon. He had married, in 1887, Lady Adela Mowbray, born 1865, daughter of the 2nd Earl of Stradbroke.

Davidson, Colonel Arthur (1856–1922); Groom-in-Waiting to Queen Victoria 1878–1901; Equerry, Assistant Keeper of the Privy Purse and Assistant Private Secretary to Edward VII; Equerry to Queen Alexandra from 1910; K.C.V.O. 1906.

Davies, Fanny; English pianist born 1861; started to play the piano when she was three years old; studied at Frankfort-on-Maine under Clara Schuman. Her first important public appearance as a solo pianist was at a Crystal Palace orchestral concert in October 1885. She played all over Europe.

de Staal, Baron Georges-Frederic (1824–1907); entered the Russian Diplomatic Service in 1845, and in 1850 was appointed attaché in Constantinople. He was Second Secretary in Athens 1859; First Secretary at Constantinople 1862, and Minister at Stuttgart, Munich, Baden and Darmstadt 1871–84. He was Ambassador in London 1884–1902. In 1879 he married Princess Sophie Gorchakova, daughter of the Adjutant General, Prince Michael Gorchakova, former High Commander of the Russian Army at Sebastopol. They had one daughter. He was very popular in England and particularly friendly with the Prince of Wales.

Donaldson, the Rev. Stuart Alexander, D.D., son of Sir S. A. Donaldson, first Premier of New South Wales; at Eton as a boy 1868–73; 1st Class Classical Tripos at Trinity College, Cambridge, 1877; assistant Master at Eton 1878–85; House Master 1885–1904; Master of Magdalene College, Cambridge, 1904–15; married in 1900 Lady Albinia Frederica, daughter of Lord Hobart and sister of the 7th Earl of Buckinghamshire; died October 1915.

Duleep Singh, Prince Victor, born 1868, grandson of Ranjit Singh (1780–1839, no relation of the cricketer), who was known as the Lion of the Punjab. Ranjit Singh consolidated most of the Punjab, was founder of the Sikh kingdom and became Maharaja of Lahore. Ranjit's son, Duleep Singh (1837–1893), who had become Maharaja under the regency of his mother, was deposed in 1849 after two anti-British risings, taken into custody and deported to England, where he lived on a government pension for the rest of his life and became a Christian. He was said to be the fourth best shot in England, and would shoot sitting down on a mat, swivelling round as if on a pivot. He had two sons, Victor and Edward, who were allowed to retain their father's courtesy title of Prince. Victor was the Queen's godson. There is a story that he referred jokingly to her as Mrs Fagin, receiver of

stolen goods, because she knew that the Koh-i-noor diamond
had been stolen from his father's palace in Lahore. In fact
Duleep Singh was "advised" by Lord Dalhousie, Governor-
General at the time of his deposition, to present it to the Queen.
Prince Victor married, in 1898, Lady Anne Coventry, daughter of
the 9th Earl of Coventry, and they had two very pretty daughters.

Edwards, Lieut-Colonel the Rt. Hon. Sir Fleetwood Isham, P.C.
(1842–1910); K.C.M.G. 1891; Assistant Keeper of the Privy
Purse and Assistant Private Secretary to Queen Victoria 1878–95;
Groom-in-Waiting 1880–95; Privy Councillor 1895; Keeper of
the Privy Purse 1895–1901; extra Equerry to Edward VII
1888–1910. He married first, in 1871, Edith Smith-Masters who
died 1873; secondly, in 1880, Mary, daughter of Major John
Routledge Majendie.

Eliot, the Very Rev. Philip, D.D., born 1835; appointed in 1891
Dean of Windsor and Domestic Chaplain to Queen Victoria.
Before his appointment he had been one of the most popular
Evangelical preachers in Bournemouth where he was for many
years rector of one of the fashionable churches. In 1883 he married
as his second wife the Hon. Mary Pitt, daughter of Lord Rivers
and until her marriage Maid-of-Honour to the Queen.

Elwin, the Rev. Whitwell (1816–1898); Rector of Booton in
Norfolk; for many years editor of the *Quarterly Review*, and
in that capacity a friend of Scott, Lockhart, Dickens, Thackeray,
Forster and Bulwer Lytton. He was a devoted friend of all the
Lytton family.

Ewart, Major-General Sir Henry, born 1838; appointed Crown
Equerry 1894. He was officially in charge of all the stables and of
all the processions. He had a very great knowledge of horses.
He was created K.C.B. in 1885, G.C.V.O. in 1902, and a Baronet
in 1910. He married, in 1888, Lady Evelyn Willoughby,
daughter of the 1st Earl of Ancaster.

Forrest, Very Rev. Robert William, M.A.; Vicar of St Jude's, South
Kensington 1879–91; Dean of Worcester 1891–1908 when he
died. His first wife died in 1903, and in 1905 he married Annie
Eisdell, widow of Ewen Hay Cameron.

Gardiner, General Sir Henry Lyndoch (1820-97), son of General
Sir Robert Gardiner; attached to Queen Victoria's Household
for twenty-four years as Groom-in-Waiting and Equerry. He
married in 1849 Frances, daughter of Francis Newdigate. He
died on December 15, 1897 and the Queen mourned him as the
last of her contemporaries "of the former happy old Claremont
days."

Glenesk, Lady and Lord. See Borthwick.

Grant, Victoria, born 1857; Maid-of-Honour to Queen Victoria
1881–84, and extra Woman-of-the-Bedchamber from 1884 when
she married Alaric Frederick Grant, a Lieutenant in the Navy.

She was a daughter of Evan Baillie and Lady Frances Bruce, daughter of the 7th Earl of Elgin.

Harbord, the Hon. Judith, born 1862, daughter of the 5th Baron Suffield and sister of Lady Carrington; appointed Maid-of-Honour to Queen Victoria in 1894. In 1901 she married the Rev. Frederick Sullivan, who succeeded in 1906 as the 7th Baronet of Thames Ditton.

Havelock, Sir Arthur (1844–1908); Governor of Ceylon 1889–95; Governor of Madras 1896–1901; K.C.B. 1884; G.C.M.G. 1895; G.C.I.E. 1896; married, in 1871, Anne, daughter of Sir William Norris.

Hohenlohe-Langenburg, Princess Victor of; widow of Prince Victor of Hohenlohe-Langenburg (1833–1891), third and youngest son of Queen Victoria's half-sister, Feodora. Princess Victor was Laura (Lolo), youngest daughter of Admiral Sir George Seymour and sister of the 5th Marquess of Hertford. Prince Victor was in the British navy but retired in 1866 owing to ill health. On his marriage in 1861, he took the second family title of Count Gleichen, as, according to German law, his wife, not being of equal rank, was disqualified from using his title of Prince, but in 1885 he was permitted to revert to his former title. He had a son, Lord Edward, and three daughters who retained the name of Gleichen.

Hollmann, Joseph; cellist born in Holland in 1852; died in Paris 1927; studied at Brussels Conservatoire, winning first prize in 1870; then at Paris Conservatoire; played at many concerts in Europe and America; lived mostly in Paris. Saint-Saëns wrote his second cello concerto for Hollmann.

Hughes, the Hon. Mary, born 1855; appointed Maid-of-Honour to Queen Victoria July 10, 1891. She was a daughter of Hugh Robert Hughes and Lady Florentia Liddell. Lady Florentia was a daughter of the 1st Earl of Ravensworth. Mary Hughes was Lady Lytton's first cousin once removed. Afterwards she was for a time Lady-in-Waiting to Princess Marie Louise.

Kennedy, John Gordon (1836–1912); Minister at Santiago 1888–98; Minister at Bucharest 1898–1905 when he retired; K.C.M.G. 1901; married, in 1877, Evelyn, daughter of Colonel the Hon. Edward Bootle-Wilbraham, a brother of Lord Lathom.

Knollys, Charlotte (1835–1930), daughter of Sir William Knollys who had been Comptroller of the Prince of Wales's Household and had retired in 1877. In 1872 she was appointed a Woman-of-the-Bedchamber to the Princess of Wales and remained the Princess's lifelong friend. Her brother, Sir Francis Knollys, who was Private Secretary to Edward VII, both as King and Prince of Wales, was created Viscount Knollys in 1911.

Lambart, the Hon. Frances (Fanny), born 1869; appointed Maid-of-Honour to Queen Victoria January 1, 1890. She was a daughter

of Gustavius Lambart, a cousin of the Earl of Cavan, and Lady
Bertha, a daughter of the 2nd Marquess Conyngham.

Lee, Henry Austin, born 1847; Private Secretary to successive
Under Secretaries of State and Ambassadors including Lord
Lytton when he was in Paris; married in 1892 Madeleine,
daughter of Benjamin Smith and widow of Arthur Taylor;
K.C.M.G. 1902.

Liddell, Geraldine (Gerry), born 1855; daughter of Colonel the
Hon. Augustus Liddell, sixth son of the 1st Baron Ravensworth,
and Cecil Wellesley, a niece of the Duke of Wellington. She
was Lady Lytton's first cousin. She was a great favourite with
all the Royal family and a particular friend of Princess Helena
Victoria (Thora). She was very musical.

Lygon, Lady Mary, born 1869, eldest daughter of the 6th Earl
Beauchamp; appointed Lady-in-Waiting to the Duchess of York
1895, and to Queen Alexandra 1901 and to Queen Mary 1910.
She married in 1905 Lieut.-Colonel the Hon. Henry Hepburn-
Stuart-Forbes-Trefusis.

Lytton, Constance (1869–1923), Lady Lytton's second daughter;
became a militant suffragette in 1908 and was imprisoned four
times; gave up public life in 1912 when she was stricken with
paralysis as a result of forcible feeding in prison. She wrote a
book about her experiences, *Prison and Prisoners*, which was
published in 1914. She never married. In 1900 she was asked to
become Lady-in-Waiting to Princess Marie Louise but declined
the honour as she did not feel she was suited to the position.

Maclagan, the Hon Augusta, born 1836, fourth daughter of the 6th
Viscount Barrington and Jane Liddell, daughter of the 1st
Baron Ravensworth. She was Lady Lytton's first cousin. In 1878
she married as his second wife William Dalrymple Maclagan,
Bishop of Lichfield, who was appointed Archbishop of York in
1891. He retired in 1908. Before her marriage Mrs Maclagan
worked under Octavia Hill and had entire charge of a London
district. She had a son and a daughter.

M'Neill, Major General Sir John Carstairs, V.C. (1831–1904);
Senior Equerry to Queen Victoria and afterwards Equerry to
Edward VII; K.C.B. 1882; G.C.V.O. 1901; unmarried.

Majendie, the Hon. Aline, born 1872, daughter of Lewis Ashurst
Majendie, who died 1885, and Lady Margaret, daughter of the
25th Earl of Crawford. She was appointed Maid-of-Honour to
Queen Victoria on 8 June 1894. In 1903 she married as his second
wife the 1st Baron Grenfell.

Mallet, Marie. *née* Adeane, born 1859; Woman-of-the-
Bedchamber to Queen Victoria, and, before her marriage, a
Maid-of-Honour, appointed 1887. She was Lady Lytton's first
cousin once removed. Her mother, who had been Lady Elizabeth
Yorke, daughter of the 4th Earl of Hardwicke, had married

Henry John Adeane, M.P. In 1891 Marie married Bernard
Mallet (1859–1932), son of Sir Louis Mallet. Bernard Mallet
was Private Secretary to Arthur Balfour when he was First Lord
of the Treasury and became Commissioner of the Inland Revenue
in 1903. He was knighted in 1916.

Monson, Augusta Louise, daughter of Lieut.-Colonel the Hon.
Augustus Ellis, son of the 1st Baron Seaford; Lady-in-Waiting
to the Duchess of Edinburgh; married in 1861 Debonnair
John Monson, Equerry, Comptroller and Treasurer to the
Duke of Edinburgh, both before and after he became Duke of
Coburg, who succeeded his brother in 1898 as 8th Baron Monson
and died in 1900. He was also a brother of Sir Edmund Monson,
Ambassador in Paris. Mrs Monson was a great linguist and a
dear friend of all the Edinburgh children as well as of their
mother. She accompanied the eldest daughter, Marie, to
Roumania when she first went there as the wife of the Crown
Prince Ferdinand.

Moore, the Hon. Evelyn, born 1856; appointed Maid-of-Honour
to Queen Victoria on March 12, 1881. She was a daughter of the
Rev. Edward Moore, Hon. Canon of Canterbury, Rector of
Frittenden in Kent, and Lady Harriet Scott, daughter of the 4th
Duke of Buccleuch. In 1901 she retired with a pension.

Mouchy, Duchesse de, *née* Princess Anna Murat, grand-daughter of
Joachim, King of Naples. She married Antoine de Noailles, Duc
de Mouchy, one of the few members of the old French nobility
to appear at the Court of Napoleon III.

Olga, Grand Duchess, born 15 November 1895, murdered 16 July
1918; eldest child of the Tsar, Nicholas II. It was a tragedy
that this beautiful and talented girl was not married and safely
out of Russia by the time the revolution came. Her parents had
tried to arrange a marriage between her and Prince Carol of
Roumania but she had not been attracted by him and was
determined to marry only for love. Other matrimonial plans
were shelved at the outbreak of war. During the war she was a
nurse in the Palace Hospital at Tsarskoe Selo.

Ottewell, B. J. Maler; honorary member of the Royal Institute of
Painters in Water Colours 1895; exhibited at the Royal Academy
between 1885 and 1892; lived at Wimbledon and died in 1937.

Paget, Walburga, Lady. Before her marriage she had been Countess
von Hohenthal and Lady-in-Waiting to the Empress Frederick
when Crown Princess. She had been instrumental in choosing Alexandra of Denmark as wife for the Prince of Wales.
She married in 1860 Sir Augustus Berkeley Paget, who was
Ambassador at Vienna from 1884–93. He had been a great
friend of Lord Lytton who was under him when he was Minister
in Copenhagen. He died in 1896.

Phipps, the Hon. Harriet, born 1841, daughter of Colonel Sir Charles

Phipps, former Keeper of the Privy Purse to Queen Victoria and second son of the 1st Earl of Mulgrave. She was a Maid-of-Honour to Queen Victoria 1862–89 and a Woman-of-the-Bedchamber 1889–1901. She was more constantly with the Queen than any of the other ladies and was in fact more an unofficial secretary than a Lady-in-Waiting. The Queen wrote about her to Sir Henry Ponsonby in 1885 that she was "very clear, quick and discreet." She was Lady Lytton's cousin by marriage, for her father was a brother of Lord Normanby who had married the eldest sister of Lady Lytton's mother.

Ponsonby, the Hon. Lady, daughter of John Crocker Bulteel of Flete, Devon, and Lady Elizabeth Grey; married in 1861 Sir Henry Ponsonby, Queen Victoria's Private Secretary; Maid-of-Honour, and, after her marriage, extra Woman-of-the-Bedchamber to the Queen. The Ponsonbys had three sons and two daughters.

Pourtalès, Madame de, *née* Melanie de Bussière; a great friend of the Lyttons when they were in Paris. She and Pauline Metternich were the Empress Eugénie's closest friends.

Probyn, General the Rt. Hon. Sir Dighton, P.C. (1833–1924), Colonel of the 11th King Edward's Own Lancers (Probyn's Horse). He had achieved a brilliant reputation as a cavalry officer in the Indian Army before he joined the Prince of Wales's Household as Equerry in 1872. In 1877 he became the Prince's Comptroller and Treasurer, and Keeper of the Privy Purse after the Prince's accession. At King Edward's death he became Comptroller of Queen Alexandra's Household and kept that position until his death. In 1872 he married Letitia, who died 1900, daughter of T. R. Thelluson.

Pugno, Raoul (1852–1914), French pianist and composer; Professor of the Conservatoire in Paris 1892–1901. He first appeared in London with a recital of his own in May 1894.

Salmond, Norman; bass singer born in Bradford 1858; studied locally; first came to notice singing in the *Messiah* at Leeds in 1886. Thereafter he sang in concerts all over England and toured in South Africa in 1895 and in America in 1896. He married an American pianist and was the father of Felix Salmond, the cellist.

Seckendorff, Count Theodor von; Chamberlain and Secretary to the Empress Frederick from 1865 until her death. He was a great art connoisseur and was himself an artist. He was an enthusiastic lover of England having spent some years there when his father was attached to the Prussian Legation in London. He died in 1910.

Singh, Duleep. See Duleep Singh.

Staal, Baron de. See de Staal.

Tufnell, Lieut.-Colonel Edward, born 1848; retired from army 1889; appointed Gentleman-at-Arms 1894; M.P. for South-East

12

Essex 1900–6; married Ellen Bertha, daughter of Rev. R. S. Gubbins.

Villiers, Edward (1806–1843), a brother of the 4th Earl of Clarendon. He was Lady Lytton's father. In 1835 he married Elizabeth Liddell after a long engagement. He held a few minor government appointments but remained very poor. He never felt well in the whole of his life and suffered from chronic depression. He died at Nice of consumption.

Villiers, Colonel Ernest (1838–1921), the only son of Edward and Elizabeth Villiers and Lady Lytton's only brother. On his retirement from the army in 1874, he became Secretary to Lord Dudley until the latter's death in 1885. He was then asked by the Duke and Duchess of Teck to become their secretary and went down to White Lodge, Richmond, where they were then living, to look into their affairs, but when he found that the butcher's bill had not been paid for twenty years he declined the honour. He first married, in 1866, Elizabeth Wood, who died in childbirth the following year; secondly, in 1869, Adela Sarah Ibbetson, daughter of Colonel Charles Ibbetson and the beautiful Lady Adela, a daughter of Lord Jersey. His daughter, Adela (1872–1956), mentioned in Lady Lytton's diary, married Sir Francis Smith in 1901.

White, Henry, born 1850; First Secretary at the American Embassy in London 1897–1905; American Ambassador to Italy 1905–7 and to France 1907–9; married first, in 1879, Margaret Rutherfurd; secondly, in 1920, Emily Vanderbilt, widow of William Douglas Sloane.

Wolff, Johannes; violinist, born 1863. Dutch by birth he spent much of his life in England and Paris and taught for some years at the Guildhall School of Music. He, like Madame Albani, was a great favourite with the Queen and a friend of Princess Marie Louise. His violin was a Guarnerius and was presented to him by the Paris Conservatoire.

Wyndham, Hugh, born 1836; Minister at Rio de Janeiro 1884–94 and at Bucharest 1894–97 when he retired. He was created K.C.M.G. in 1894 and received the Diamond Jubilee medal in 1897. In 1863 he married Charlotte Elizabeth, daughter of the Rev. the Hon. William Scott, son of the 4th Baron Polworth.

Yorke, the Hon. Alexander Grantham (Alick) (1847–1911), younger son of the 4th Earl of Hardwicke. His mother had been the Hon. Susan Liddell, daughter of the 1st Baron Ravensworth. He was Lady Lytton's first cousin. He was appointed Gentleman-in-Waiting to Queen Victoria in 1884, having previously been Equerry to the Duke of Albany. As an enthusiastic amateur actor, he produced and acted in all the amateur theatricals performed before the Queen while he was in waiting. He was created C.V.O. in 1901 when he became an extra Groom-in-Waiting to Edward VII.

Books Consulted

Albani, Emma: *Forty Years of Song* (1911).

Annual Register, The (1895–1901).

Anonymous: *Uncensored Recollections* (1924).

Armytage, Percy: *By the Clock of St James's* (1927).

Askwith, Lord: *Lord James of Hereford* (1930).

Balfour, Betty: *Letters of Constance Lytton* (1925).

Balfour, Betty: *Personal and Literary Letters of the Earl of Lytton* (1906).

Barclay, Florence: *Through the Postern Gate* (1912).

Barkeley, Richard: *The Empress Frederick* (1956).

Benson, E. F.: *The Kaiser and English Relations* (1936).

Benson, E. F.: *Queen Victoria* (1935).

Benson, E. F.: *Daughters of Queen Victoria* (1939).

Blunt, Wilfrid Scawen: *My Diaries, 1888–1900* (1919).

Bolitho, Hector: *Further Letters of Queen Victoria* (1938).

Brown, Ivor: *Balmoral* (1955).

Buchanan, Meriel: *Queen Victoria's Relations* (1954).

Bulygin, Captain: *The Murder of the Romanovs* (1935).

Buxhoeveden, Baroness Sophie: *The Life and Tragedy of Alexandra Feodorovna* (1928).

Chapman, Guy: *The Dreyfus Case* (1955).

Collier, E. C. F. (editor): *A Victorian Diarist, Extracts from the Journals of Mary, Lady Monkswell, 1873–1895* (1944), and *Further Extracts, 1895–1909* (1946).

Corti, Egon Caesar, Conte: *Alexander von Battenberg*, translated by E. M. Hodgson (1954).

Country Life (1897–1901).

Daily Courier, The, (1897).

Debrett.

Dictionary of National Biography, The.

Duff, David: *The Shy Princess* (1958).

Filon, Augustin: *Recollections of the Empress Eugenie* (1920).

179

Florinsky, Mikhail T.: *Russia, a History and an Interpretation,* (Volume 2) (1955).

Gilliard, Pierre: *Thirteen Years at the Russian Court* (1931).

Greece, Prince Christopher of: *Memoirs* (1938).

Hanbury-Williams, Sir John: *The Emperor Nicholas II as I knew Him* (1922).

Hassall, Christopher: *Edward Marsh* (1959).

Hussey, Christopher: *The Life of Sir Edwin Lutyens* (1950).

Lady's Realm, The, Volumes 1–14.

Lee, Arthur Gould: *The Empress Frederick Writes to Sophie* (1950).

Lee, Sidney: *King Edward VII* (Volume I) (1925).

Lee, Sidney: *Queen Victoria* (1902).

Letters of the Tsar to the Tsaritsa, 1914–17, edited by A. L. Hynes (1929).

Letters of Tsar Nicholas and Empress Marie, edited by J. Bing (1937).

Letters of the Tsaritsa to the Tsar, 1914–16 (1923).

Lutyens, Lady Emily: *A Blessed Girl* (1953).

Lutyens, Lady Emily: *The Birth of Rowland* (1956).

McAlister, Isabel: *Alfred Gilbert* (1929).

Marie Louise, Princess: *My Memories of Six Reigns* (1957).

Marsh, Edward: *A Number of People* (1939).

Mossolov, A. A.: *The Court of the Last Tsar* (1935).

Osborne House (Ministry of Works).

Paget, Walburga Lady: *Embassies of Other Days* (1923).

Pearson, Hesketh: *Gilbert and Sullivan* (1935).

Ponsonby, Arthur: *Henry Ponsonby* (1943).

Ponsonby, Frederick: *Recollections of Three Reigns* (1951).

Ponsonby, Frederick: *Sidelights on Queen Victoria* (1930).

Pope-Hennessy, James: *Queen Mary* (1959).

Pope-Hennessy, James: *Queen Victoria at Windsor and Balmoral* (1959).

Punch (1895–1901).

Radziwill, Princess Catherine: *The Empress Frederick* (1934).

Radziwill, Princess Catherine: *Intimate Life of the Last Tsarina* (1929).

Radziwill, Princess Catherine: *Nicholas II, the Last of the Tsars* (1931).

Radziwill, Princess Catherine: *The Taint of the Romanovs* (1931).

Roumania, Queen Marie of: *The Story of My Life* (1934).

Russia, Grand Duchess Marie of: *Things I Remember* (1930).

Slatin Pasha: *Fire and Sword in the Soudan* (1896).

Stevenson, R. Scott: *Morell Mackenzie* (1946).

Tisdall, E. E. P.: *The Prince Imperial* (1959).

Turner, E. S.: *The Court of St James's* (1959).

Victoria, Queen: *Leaves from the Journal of a Life in the Highlands* (1868) and *More Leaves from the Journal of a Life in the Highlands* (1884).

Victoria, Queen: *Letters* (Second and Third Series) (1926–8, 1930–2).

Villiers, George: *Vanished Victorians* (1935).

Walsh, E. A.: *The Fall of the Russian Empire* (1929).

Whitaker's Almanack.

Whitaker's Peerage.

Who Was Who.

Wingate, Ronald: *Wingate of the Sudan* (1955).

Youssoupoff, Prince Felix: *Lost Splendour* (1953).

Showing in bold type those relations mentioned in her diary

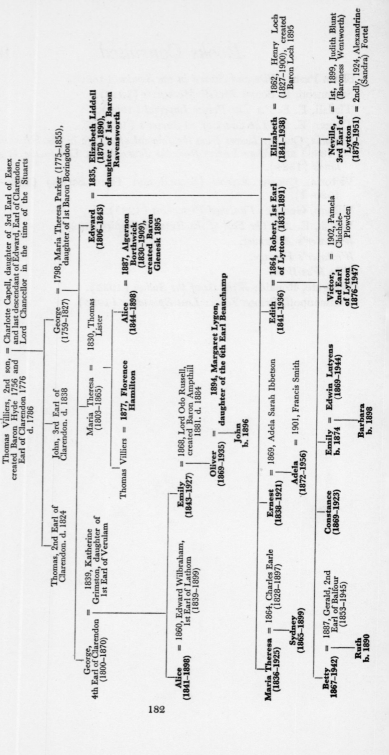

LADY LYTTON'S FAMILY TREE ON HER MOTHER'S SIDE

Showing in bold type those relations mentioned in her diary

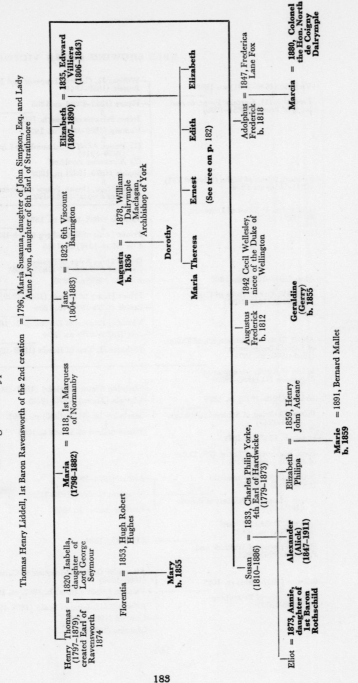

183

Victoria
(1819–1901)
m. 1840
||
Prince Albert
of Saxe-Coburg-
Gotha
(1819–1861)

—Victoria (1840–1901) m. 1858
||
Frederick III, German Emperor and
King of Prussia (1831–1888)

—William II, German Emperor and King of
Prussia (1859–1941)

—Henry (1862–1929) m. 1888
||
Irène, Princess of Hesse b. 1866

—Victoria (1866–1929) m. 1890
||
(1) Prince Adolf of Schaumburg-Lippe
(1859–1916)
(2) Alexander Zoubkoff

—Sophie (1870–1932) m. 1889
||
Constantine, Crown Prince of Greece
(Duke of Sparta) (1863–1923)

—Edward, Prince of Wales (Edward VII)
(1841–1910) m. 1863
||
Alexandra, Princess of Denmark
(1844–1925)

—Alice (1843–1878) m. 1862
||
Louis IV, Grand Duke of Hesse-
Darmstadt (1837–1892)

—Victoria (1863–1950) m. 1884
||
Prince Louis of Battenberg (1854–1921)

—Ella (1864–1918) m. 1886
||
Grand Duke Serge of Russia
(uncle of Nicholas II) (1857–1905)

—Irène b. 1866, m. 1888
||
Prince Henry of Prussia (1862–1929)

—Ernest (1868–1937) m. 1894
||
Victoria, Princess of Edinburgh b. 1876

—Alix (1872–1918) m. 1894
||
Nicholas II, Tsar of Russia (1868–1918)

—Alfred, Duke of Edinburgh and Duke
of Saxe-Coburg-Gotha
(1844–1900) m. 1874
||
Marie of Russia (daughter of
Alexander II) (1853–1920)

—Helena (1846–1923) m. 1866
||
Prince Christian of Schleswig-Holstein
(1831–1917)

—Christian Victor (Christle) (1867–1900)

—Victoria (Thora) (1870–1948)

—Marie Louise (1872–1956) m. 1891
||
Prince Aribert of Anhalt b. 1864

—Louise b. 1848, m. 1871
||
John, Marquess of Lorne (9th Duke
of Argyll) (1845–1914)

—Arthur, Duke of Connaught
(1850–1942) m. 1879
||
Louise Margaret, Princess of Prussia
(1860–1917)

—Arthur (1883–1943)

—Margaret (Daisy) (1882–1920)

—Patricia (Patsy) b. 1886

—Leopold, Duke of Albany
(1853–1884) m. 1882
||
Helen, Princess of Waldeck and
Pyrmont (1861–1922)

—Charles b. 1884

—Beatrice (1857–1944) m. 1885
||
Prince Henry of Battenberg
(1958–1896)

—Alexander (Drino), Marquess of Carisbrooke
(1886–1960)

—Victoria Eugénie (Ena) b. 1887, m. 1906
||
Alfonso XIII, King of Spain (1886–1931)

—Leopold (1889–1922)

—Maurice (1891–1914)

—————————————————————— Waldemar b. 1889
—Albert Victor, Duke of Clarence (1864–1892)
—George, Duke of York (George V) (1865–1936)　　—Edward (Duke of Windsor) b. 1894
　‖　　　　　　　　　　　　　　　　　　　　　├—Albert (George VI) (1895–1952)
　Princess Mary of Teck (1867–1953)　　　　　　—Mary b. 1897
—Louise (1867–1931) m. 1889
　‖　　　　　　　　　　　　　　　　　—Alexandra (1891–1959)
　Duke of Fife (1849–1912)　　　　　　　└—Maud (1893–1945)
—Victoria (1868–1935)
—Maud (1869–1938) m. 1896
　‖
　Prince Charles of Denmark (Haakon VII of
　Norway) (1872–1957)

————————————————————————— Alice b. 1885　　　——————— Philip
　　　　　　　　　　　　　　　　　　　　　　　　　　‖　　　　　　　　　　　　(Duke of
　　　　　　　　　　　　　　　　　　　　　　　Prince Andrew　　　　　　Edinburgh)
　　　　　　　　　　　　　　　　　　　　　　　of Greece　　　　　　　　b. 1921

————————————————————————— Waldemar b. 1889

————————————————————————— Elizabeth (1895–1903)

————————————————————————— Olga (1895–1918)

—Alfred (1874–1899)

—Marie b. 1875, m. 1893
　‖　　　　　　　　　　　　　　　　—————— Carol b. 1893
　Ferdinand of Roumania (1865–1927)
—Victoria (Ducky) b. 1876, m. 1894
　‖　　　　　　　　　　　　　　　　—————— Elizabeth (1895–1903)
　Ernest, Grand Duke of Hesse-Darmstadt
　　(1868–1937)
—Alexandra (1878–1942) m. 1896
　‖
　Ernest, Prince of Hohenlohe-Langenburg
　　(1863–1950)

TREE SHOWING QUEEN VICTORIA'S RELATIONSHIP WITH COBURGS, HOHENLOHES AND GLEICHENS

All those shown in bold type are mentioned in the diary

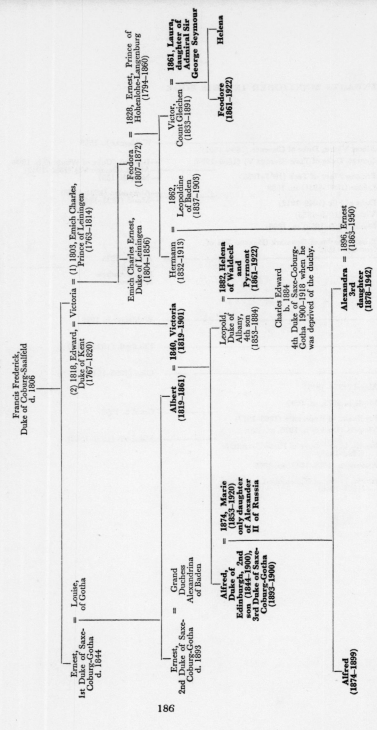

186

Index

Those included in the Biographical Index are marked with an asterisk.

187

Index